The Questioning Child and Religion

Edith Fisher Hunter is the author of *The Family Finds Out,* a book for five- and six-year-olds. A graduate of Wellesley College and Union Theological Seminary, she is a Curriculum Editor for the Division of Education, Council of Liberal Churches (Universalist-Unitarian).

THE QUESTIONING CHILD
AND RELIGION

EDITH F. HUNTER

THE STARR KING PRESS   **BOSTON**

Distributed by

The Beacon Press, 25 Beacon Street, Boston 8

The poem "Vespers" by A. A. Milne, quoted in Chapter 9, is from *When We Were Very Young* (copyright 1924 by E. P. Dutton & Co., Inc., renewal 1952 by A. A. Milne).

First printing, September 1956

Second printing, October 1956

Contents

PART TWO

Foreword

Alfred North Whitehead once wrote, "The vitality of religion is shown by the way in which the religious spirit has survived the ordeal of religious education."[1] Happily, for the sake of our children, many of us have found that it is possible for religious education to be something other than an ordeal.

This is true, in no small measure, because of the pioneering work of Sophia Lyon Fahs. Mrs. Fahs not only has developed a philosophy to undergird a new approach to religious education, but also has been largely responsible for the preparation of a library of books that are needed tools for parents and teachers adventuring in this new way.

The present book has been written out of a need created by the use of this fresh approach. My three children and I were finding how real and exciting religious education can be. But I soon discovered that a deep division existed between the vital experiences and broad excursions in thought that we were enjoying and felt to be "religious," and the phenomena which my children found labeled "religious" by our society. How could this gap be bridged? How could I make its existence intelligible to my children? How could I help them live with it?

From various reports, I felt sure that other parents and teachers adventuring in the new ways were confronted by this same problem. The Division of Education of the Council of Liberal Churches (Universalist-Unitarian) distributed a

---

[1] Reference notes begin on page 203.

questionnaire among liberal religious parents and teachers in church schools in various parts of the country. The questionnaire requested accounts of actual experiences and conversations with children, relating to the conflict between a liberal and a traditional approach to religious education.

We were especially interested in conversations on the subjects of God, Jesus, prayer, the Bible, Heaven, Hell, death, traditional festivals, and different religious practices. We asked for a description of the context of the discussion, what emotion the child showed, what emotion the parent or adult felt. We requested relevant background information for the conversation. And we asked how both the adult and the child seemed to feel as a result of the whole incident. We also inquired whether the adult would handle the situation in the same manner another time.

The ninety responses to this questionnaire reassured me that mine was a common problem. Indeed many of the problems discussed in these pages confront orthodox as well as liberal religious parents. I am greatly indebted to the persons who took the time and thought necessary to report these conversations. The insight gained from them, as well as many of the cases they reported, are scattered throughout this book. Names have been altered in many instances, and also certain details. I wish also to thank here many persons with whom I have talked over this problem in informal conversations.

The book has also benefited, in an earlier form, from the careful and critical reading of a number of persons. For nearly ten years, Mrs. Fahs has listened, largely through the mail, as I wrestled with many of the ideas in this book. She gave the manuscript itself careful criticism. I also wish to thank the following friends for wonderfully helpful and thorough comments: Mrs. Dorothy T. Spoerl and Miss Lucile Lindberg, both Curriculum Editors for the Division of Education of the Council of Liberal Churches (Universalist-Unitarian); Dr. Ivar Hellstrom, formerly of Riverside Church,

New York; Mrs. Katherine Wensberg of Mercer Island, Seattle, Washington; Mrs. Jean Hueston of Zenith, Washington; and Mrs. Caroline Courts of Mansfield, Massachusetts. I am also grateful to the following members of the Curriculum Committee of the Division of Education of the Council of Liberal Churches: Mrs. Elizabeth Manwell, Mrs. Florence Klaber, Miss Marguerite Hallowell, Mrs. Amelia Swayne, and Dr. Ernest W. Kuebler. All of these critics will perhaps take exception to some parts of the book as it now stands, but I am nonetheless greatly in the debt of all of them. The Field Workers of the Division of Education, Miss Frances W. Wood and Rev. Edna P. Bruner, have kept me keenly aware of the kinds of situations that parents and teachers are facing in this area. I would also like to thank Mrs. Mary Jane Goodfellow for typing an early draft of the manuscript.

This book cannot offer neat solutions to our dilemma, both because of the nature of the problem and because of my limited experience and insight. But sometimes it helps simply to describe a common problem. Perhaps the book will serve as a stimulus to clearer thought and better solutions.

The "we" used throughout the book is usually an editorial we, referring only to myself, yet used with the conviction that many parents and teachers may feel it speaks for them.

There are some inconsistencies in the book, and several theoretical problems are raised for which I still know no solution. For this, and for perhaps a note of too much certitude, I must apologize. But I write with the zeal and lack of leisure of a practitioner in the new way — not as a theorist.

For my deepest thanks belong to my own family. My daughter Elizabeth, now ten, was six when the problem of the book was forced into my mind. Without her questions and her insight, there would be no book. My eight-year-old son Graham, impatient with cant or pretense, keeps my theological feet on the ground. My husband has joined in excursions of thought when the children are tucked into bed. My own parents have always encouraged and stimulated my thinking.

The new directions this kind of religious education may take and the further problems it will entail await discovery and analysis. Much valuable research can be done at home by alert parents who are as ready to learn from children as to teach them.

I am glad that I am going to have to start all over again in religious education. For as my husband started off to church on a recent Sunday, our two-year-old son William asked, "Where's him going?"

"To church," I said.

"Whuz him going to get there?" asked William.

I could see the line of thought. At the store we get food; at the lumber yard we get lumber; at the station we get Daddy. But what do we get at church? Children ask perplexing questions. How shall we answer them?

E. F. H.

THE QUESTIONING CHILD AND RELIGION

1

The Culture Will Not Wait

"But, Mother, how did they kill Jesus?"

"Mother," said four-year-old Graham, running in from his play in the yard, "did Jesus get killed?"

I was busy stirring a pudding on the stove. "Yes," I said slowly, "Jesus did get killed."

"Why did he get killed?" asked the little boy.

It was just before Good Friday. Apparently Graham had heard from his playmates in the yard something that puzzled him.

With some uneasiness I tried to arrange my thoughts. I felt that my answer would be the beginning of our son's understanding of the significance of Jesus' life. I felt that the subject was something much too big for a four-year-old to grapple with, but I wanted to give him all the help I could.

"They killed Jesus," I answered carefully, "because some people did not like what he was teaching."

And then I wondered what this reference to teaching would mean to Graham. He sometimes played school with his six-year-old sister, she as teacher and he as pupil. She taught him numbers and letters. This is all that Graham knew about teaching. It would be hard for him to see why anyone would be killed for doing that.

There was something else that Graham wanted to know, and I had not answered it yet. "But, Mother, how did they kill Jesus?" Graham asked.

I hesitated. "Well, they killed him in a way that they some-

1

times killed people in those days," I said, hoping that this would satisfy him.

"How?" persisted Graham. It was clear to me now that he had already heard from his playmates the answer to his own question, and it was something he wanted straight from me.

"It was a cruel way. They put his body on a long board and stretched his arms out on another board that went across it, and stuck the whole thing up in the ground."

"How did he stay up on it?" asked Graham.

"They put nails through his hands and feet," I said. I took the pudding off the stove.

"Oh," he said and walked away.

I had plans for Graham's religious education. To have him hear, at the age of four, about the crucifixion of Jesus was not a part of my plan. I belong to a large and growing group of parents, teachers, and ministers discontented with the old ways of teaching religion and eagerly experimenting with new ways.

We believe that religion has its natural roots in the everyday living of children. Therefore, we wish to begin by making sure that our children are having rich experiences in the here and now, instead of beginning by telling them stories about Jesus or the ancient Hebrew heroes who lived so long ago and far away.

Young children should have experiences with wind and sun and rain, with seeds and flowers and fruit, with insect life and animal life and human life, with birth and growth and death. Out of such experiences, and man's grappling with them, all religions have sprung.

We believe that children should first be helped to reflect on such experiences in their own words, before being given adult ideas and explanations. Little children should be encouraged to express their wonder, fear, enthusiasm, questionings in their own spontaneous ways, rather than being taught traditional ways of ritual and prayer.

Encouraging them to plumb the depths of their here-and-now experiences is a sound way to start children on the high road to a mature religion. In due time, they will study and compare with their own searchings the religious gropings of men of other times and places.

An ever-growing library of books is being developed to help parents, teachers, and ministers guide the religious growth of children along these lines.[1] Free of the unreality and confusion that so often marks the old ways in religious education, this new way is being welcomed enthusiastically by a growing number of liberal religious adults and their children.

Many parents and teachers have started out eagerly in this new way, only to be rudely confronted, as I was, with other kinds of equally real here-and-now experiences — that is, experiences with traditional religious ideas and practices. For our children hear some perplexing things about religion in their contacts with other children. Graham's was no isolated case.

Barbara and Billy were climbing trees while Billy's mother pared apples. Barbara, who was five years old, was standing on the topmost branch of a low box elder tree, "right next to the sky," as she put it. Billy, who was also five, was climbing nearby.

Looking up into the clouds, Barbara announced suddenly, "Jesus is up there. He's magic. I could say, 'Jesus,' and jump down to the ground, and it wouldn't hurt, because he's so magic."

"He must be Superman," said Bill, swinging down to the ground from a low branch. "Mother, was Jesus magic?"

Or there was the evening Betsy was in the bathtub scrubbing her knees. She was six years old and in the first grade.

"Sally said God is in her church," said Betsy.

"Oh," replied her father, "did she?"

"Sally's Catholic," said Betsy. "She said God isn't in any other churches, just Catholic!"

"That's what some of them believe," said Daddy.

"Is he?" asked Betsy.

"What do you think?" queried her father.

"I don't know," said Betsy. "I don't even know exactly what God is. I don't think God is a person that can *be* anywhere. Sally makes me mad — she's so bossy!" And Betsy went off on a tirade about Sally.

Such questions as these are asked not only as a result of talk with playmates and classmates, but also from a variety of contacts both inside and outside the home.

Six-year-old Mike, child of liberal Jewish parents, came back from a neighbor's house. "Daddy, who is God? And why do the Schweitzers want to know if we are Jewish?"

The Schweitzers were orthodox Jews. Mike's father asked his son to explain just what had happened.

"Well," said Mike, "Harry's uncle, who was there, asked if I was a good Jewish boy and if I believed in God and prayed to him. Why did he want to know?"

A seven-year-old girl returned home from a visit with a friend. They had been to the friend's Bible school. After an hour spent quietly in the living room, the little girl suddenly and firmly made an announcement to her father and mother.

"I'm going to the movies every Sunday afternoon."

For a moment her father and mother sat in a slightly stunned silence.

Then her father asked, "Why are you going to the movies every Sunday afternoon?"

"Then Jesus won't get me. At Bible school the teacher said that someday Jesus was coming down from Heaven, and he would take each of us in his arms and carry us up to Heaven one by one."

"But why won't Jesus get you at the movies?" asked her father, still rather perplexed.

"Because the teacher said that Jesus would *never* go to the movies on Sunday. He couldn't get me if I was in the movies. Why did she say Jesus would do that? He couldn't really do it — could he, Daddy?"

Grandparents, neighbors, baby sitters, maids, even public-school teachers may introduce the teachings of various religious groups to our children. So, too, may books, magazines, advertisements, movies, television programs.

A young father sat in his living room one Sunday afternoon, watching, mystified, the actions of his five-year-old son and three-year-old daughter. They moved from hassock to coffee table, mumbling, raising their arms, lowering their heads; back and forth they went. Finally he asked them what they were doing.

"Like the men in the dresses on television," said the five-year-old, remembering a televised Roman Catholic mass. "What were they doing, Daddy?"

Even so untheological a book as a mail-order catalog, favorite reading of many a nine- or ten-year-old, may launch parent and child into a theological discussion. A nine-year-old girl was poring over the new Christmas catalog in the living room one evening. Suddenly she asked her father a question.

"What do you think is the greatest story you ever heard?"

The father, noting the reading matter, wondered what piece of merchandise had brought on this question.

"You'll have to give me time to think," he said. "There are

so many kinds of stories; some are great in one way, and some are great in another. I just can't say right off which is the greatest."

"Well, it says here in an ad for books: *'The Greatest Story Ever Told*. Two dollars and seventy-nine cents. Shipping weight one pound. The story of the life of Jesus.' Why do they call that the greatest story ever told?"

Peter, who was ten, had been to see the movie *David and Bathsheba* and came home very much upset over one incident in the picture. This was the point at which the ark was being carried into the city on a cart and God had said he would smite dead anyone who touched it.

"I don't think very much of God for killing the man who only touched it to keep it from falling to the ground. That's stupid. That isn't the kind of God I believe in. Do you, Mother?"

"No," said Mother. "That isn't the way I think about God."

"But did the man really die, Mother? He did in the movie."

Traditional religion often confronts our children at the most unexpected moments. Jewish-Christian history, myths, rituals, symbols, songs, holidays, sectarian divisions and controversies run all through our culture. Traditional ideas of God, formal ways of praying, the figure of Jesus, the Bible as a special book, the ideas of Heaven, Hell, sin, the Devil are inescapably a part of the world in which our children must grow up. Even our language and our ways of thinking bear the imprint of the Jewish-Christian world picture.

There is a great deal in the Jewish-Christian heritage that we want our children to understand and appreciate, and a great deal that they must someday test by their own experience and evaluate for themselves. We cannot ignore this heritage, nor do we wish to. But, because of our understanding of how children develop, we would prefer to delay the study of abstract concepts, historical material, and formalized religious practices until our children have enough experience and sufficient emotional and mental maturity to understand and evaluate this kind of material.

Our culture, however, will not wait. As early as three and four years of age, our children begin to come to us with their questions and their confused feelings about religion. Children must inevitably discover that there are many different kinds of religious beliefs and practices in our religiously free society.

It is especially important that we stand ready to help our children in the early school years, when they are first entering the larger culture. Our society bombards children with ideas and values through signs, symbols, pictures, slogans. Until they have built up a core of experience out of which to interpret this material, and until they can read easily (generally not before the fourth grade), they may be confused, misinformed, worried, and overwhelmed by the meanings that do not get through to them.

The religious education that many liberal religious parents plan for their children is radically different from the kind of religious education that many of their friends are being given and the kind that our culture takes for granted; therefore, we have an extra responsibility to try to interpret the situation to them. Many of us are increasingly confident of the soundness of our new ways in religious education and feel that teaching *about* religion is not the real job of religious education in the years from three to ten. But we also realize that we must work out ways of relating our planned program to the existing cultural situation.

Many liberal religious parents are asking: How can we help our children have not only a creative religious education but also some kind of education about traditional religion?

2

Our Own Feelings About Traditional Religion

"It took me six years to fight my way through from an orthodox position to a liberal position."

When our children come to us with their questions about traditional religion, they may find that they have touched upon an area where feelings run high. Although we may take pride in our intellectual open-mindedness about religion, we usually hold our religious position with considerable emotion.

Perhaps, therefore, it would be well for liberal religious parents and teachers to do a little self-analysis in this area. Of course, we want to be spirited liberals, capable of holding our position warmly and convincingly, but we want the warmth to stem from our positive convictions, not from negative feelings about traditional religion. Unless we clarify our own feelings, our unexamined emotions may hamper us when we are trying to help our children. We may find ourselves either unable to speak frankly with them or unduly scornful and resentful of any position other than our own.

Why do religious liberals sometimes feel a surge of emotion when children ask their questions? There are several possible causes for this reaction: the fact that many of us have come out of conservative religious homes; the isolated position in which many religious liberals find themselves; and finally the fact that the religious character of our position is often not recognized as "religious" by those holding a conservative position.

Let us consider each of these three factors.

Many religious liberals are rebels from orthodox religious homes. One mother writes: "It took me six years (from the age of twenty to twenty-six) to fight my way through from an orthodox position to a liberal position. I'll admit I was a stubborn case."

This mother would probably acknowledge that the scars of her six-year "battle" show when her children ask questions about traditional religion. She may resent their interest in something that it took her years to throw off. A question that to an inquiring child may seem simple and uncomplicated is necessarily something far more complex to the parent who hears the question against the background of his own personal conflict.

Six-year-old Henry, on coming home from school, reported a disturbing experience. "The teacher told us that God sees everything we do, so we had better behave ourselves. She said He writes it down in a book. How can He watch everyone at once?"

His mother writes: "This idea so frightened me when I was a child that I had to discard the whole concept of God before I could reconstruct any kind of religion by which to live. It is an idea that I hoped my child would never hear." For a parent with this background, to be confronted suddenly with such a question is a disturbing experience.

Our feelings may flare up even more if the ideas are introduced to our children by the very persons involved in our own rebellion. It is an added difficulty if we have heavy guilt feelings in relation to these people.

One mother writes: "My two girls, six and four, seem to take a malignant sort of pleasure in insisting on 'saying their prayers' (very orthodox ones) after every visit to Grandmother (my mother). She makes a point of teaching them these prayers and tells them that I said them when I was a little girl. It makes me boil, especially since they feel so *good* when doing it. It makes me feel like a little girl again, and a naughty one at that."

Unless this young woman can work out her relationship with her mother and at the same time clarify her own thinking on the question of children and prayer, her confused feelings and ideas will stand in the way as she tries to guide the religious development of her children and help them with their questions.

A father writes: "My sister, who has remained true to the faith of our fathers, gave my two daughters, five and three, the Petershams' book *The Christ Child* for Christmas. I was unable to intercept the present and had to sit by helplessly as they opened it and pored fascinated over the pictures. They came to the picture of the angry Herod.

" 'Why is that man so mad-looking?' they asked.

"I felt just as mad as Herod looked. Every fight I ever had with my bossy older sister flashed across my mind. Here we were having another one at the expense of my children. She knows my liberal ideas about religion. I brushed the children's question off somehow, but they knew something irritated me. Not a very good introduction to the life of Jesus and certainly not the kind I had planned!"

Here was a father, almost compulsive in his negative feelings in an area in which he wished to be positive.

We should therefore ask ourselves: Are the questions of our children an invitation to further battle, or have we gained a degree of maturity in our feelings about our rebellion against traditional religious ideas? Are we able to examine these ideas with the children's need foremost rather than our own?

A second reason for an over-emotional reaction to our children's queries may be the sense of isolation that many religious liberals report. We are living in a period of history when, in our country at least, a liberal religious position is a minority position and one that is often suspect. The emphasis of our culture is on saying the "right" thing in most controversial areas, including religion. Even the humanist and the atheist must now pledge allegiance to one nation "under God."

However, there is a growing number of people throughout the world who cannot identify themselves with traditional churches but who feel that life has a depth and breadth that should be explored and freshly expressed. In India, Japan, America, and elsewhere, there are liberal religious spirits eager to develop an inclusive religion — one that can bring people from the whole world together, as the competing orthodoxies with their exclusive dogmas never can. Though we are minorities in our several countries, we make a sizeable and growing band of positive religious liberals. We need to make ourselves known to one another and to feel the inspiration of being members in a very real and growing fellowship.

Admitting, then, that ours is a minority position in the world at large, what about the immediate situation in the homes and local communities in which each of us must live and work from day to day? Are we isolated here, too?

It is, of course, a great help if, within the home, both parents approach experience with a common religious philosophy. We believe that religion should bind people together, and surely it should begin to do this in the home. If father and mother wholeheartedly stand together, this fact will strengthen their children's religion and help them to accept a minority role in the larger community.

When people from different religious backgrounds marry, they sometimes discover that a liberal religious philosophy is the ideal solution to their dilemma. Instead of avoiding all religious questions in order to maintain harmony, and instead of continuing a state of warfare in the home as each parent clings to his orthodox beliefs, they are able to explore together the richness of the all-encompassing reality that defies any narrow definition.

In many homes no such happy solution is worked out. If only one parent is a religious liberal, he may feel a heightened need to be on the defensive about religion, for the orthodox partner has much of the community opinion behind him. But the liberal parent should take heart. Though the narrow dogmas of orthodoxy may appear convincing, definite, or appealing because they are the majority opinion, the growing child will increasingly find his first-hand experience forcing him to question authoritarian dogmas, to use his own mind, and to grow.

A liberal religious mother married to a Roman Catholic reported the following conversation between her husband and their seven-year-old son. The boy was attending instruction in preparation for first communion.

"The sister lied today. She said Jesus could stand there and tell a mountain to move, and it would. She lied because no one can do that."

His father said, "Perhaps the sister merely thought Jesus could do that. She wasn't lying if she really thought so."

The mother writes: "My son seemed to feel that anyone should be able to see the nonsense of the nun's statement. I think my husband said the only possible thing which would preserve the authority of the nun and yet not deny the boy's rational statement. I try not to correct what seems to be completely wrong in the children's Catholic instruction. If they ask me directly, I explain my viewpoint, emphasizing that what I think is not what everyone agrees with. In conversations such as this, it is at least clear to our son that people disagree about these things and that he has his own first-hand experience to take into consideration. It strengthens me to know that reality stands behind me and that it is stronger than all the man-made dogmas in the world."

Liberal religious parents in such mixed marriages are in a difficult situation when their children ask questions about traditional religion, because so many other values are involved. It is tragic when children are used as a battlefield for theological differences. We should stress at such times that these questions are matters that adults all over the world have always differed on and that a full understanding of these differences only comes gradually and as one grows up. We should emphasize that it is all right to have different ideas about these things.

We might say something like this: "Father and Mother love and respect each other, and yet think very differently about religion. You will gradually come to have your thoughts about these things, too. Perhaps someday you will find you agree with Mother or Father, or perhaps you will think quite differently from either of us."

The presence in the home of grandparents or helpers with different religious beliefs from our own will need to be handled in much the same way. Such an attitude will lessen *our* negative and defensive reactions and will lighten the worried feelings children may have because of the religious differences.

Outside the home, religious liberals may feel a sense of isolation in the community in which they live. Numerous parents reporting their concern mention that they are the only religious liberals within "ten blocks," or within "forty miles," or that their child is the "only one in the class at school." Isolation from other religious liberals may create more pressing problems for children than for adults; if there is no liberal church for the parents, there is no liberal church school for the children.

For us adults, any social isolation that may result from a liberal viewpoint is of our own choosing and for reasons we

can understand. Children, on the other hand, cannot understand the abstract and historical ideas involved in the choice
of a church affiliation. But they *can* understand that their
sense of isolation, of "being different," is *not* of their own
choosing. They may therefore resent and apparently reject
our point of view. This in turn may increase the parents'
feelings of being on the defensive.

Some religious liberals are evolving ways of dealing with
this situation. Because sensitive parents are aware of this
pressure on their children, they are searching in their immediate neighborhoods to find other liberal religious families.
They may establish small groups — or "fellowships" — under
lay leadership. Such groups soon organize small religious
schools for their children. Since lay leadership makes lay
people active, the membership often increases rapidly; a
number of these fellowships become churches. In at least
one denomination, a church-by-mail has been organized with
a church school for isolated families.[1]

Many liberal parents welcome such programs because they
find the role of the isolated liberal religious family a hard
one. Without some contact with like-minded persons, it is
dangerously easy either to become critical and bitter or
quietly to conform for the sake of community acceptance.

Sometimes religious liberals exclude themselves and their
children from the social groups of the majority in a town because they think religious ideas really matter — while members of more orthodox groups may be quite ignorant of the
religious ideas that have supposedly brought them together.

A mother in such a situation writes: "I was talking about
religion with a friend, a member of one of the orthodox
Protestant churches in town. She volunteered that, as for
religion, she didn't know anything about it and guessed she
never would, since she wasn't much interested.

" 'Well,' I said, 'how did you happen to have your two
little boys baptized last Sunday?'

" 'What do you mean?' she asked.

" 'How could you stand up and promise to try to raise them in a Christian home and to be followers of Jesus, as you did, if you don't know anything about it?'

" 'My goodness,' she said, 'I never thought of it that way. You go over to the Town Hall to get their birth certificate, and I always thought you went over to the church to have them baptized. It's just something you do. I never thought what it meant.'

"I felt a little foolish," reports the liberal mother, "when I thought of how diligently I had *not* had our children baptized at that church because of what it is supposed to mean."

Although church leaders often assert that churches ought not to function predominantly as social clubs, in many communities they do so. Recent studies show that people often affiliate with churches in new communities for this reason. This is not necessarily something to be deplored. Churches fill a real religious need for people merely by bringing them together. Man is a social being and his spirit is enriched by joining with others.

But in the orthodox churches there is a gap between the theological ground that is supposed to be the basis of fellowship and the actual ground. In many churches, commonly shared ideas about religion are seldom a subject for conversation. Indeed the ideas that are actually shared may not be theological at all, but economic, political, and social.

Another isolated liberal religious mother reports: "All my friends go to the orthodox church in town. I know them through our cooperative nursery and the P.T.A. They never discuss religion. The only women I ever discuss religion with are the one Mormon in town, a Swedenborgian, and a Seventh Day Adventist. I have a feeling that my other friends, with whom I generally feel more at ease, don't think it is 'nice' to talk about religion."

This brings us to the third factor that may lie behind an over-emotional reaction when children come with their questions. Because of the unusual content and method of our religious philosophy, our "religiousness" is difficult for others to identify, particularly if we are in a situation where there is no liberal religious church in town. Thus we may feel more on the defensive than some of the other religious minorities. Indeed we may find that if the religious label we wear is little known, or if we prefer to wear none, our friends and neighbors may conclude that we have no *religion* at all and that our children therefore have none.

A mother writes: "A problem for us is that of the adult who comes into our home as a baby sitter. She is excellent in many ways, but she insists without consulting us that she teach the children to pray when left alone with them. I have not thought we could tell her our point of view concerning religion. She would not understand, and to insist she do nothing would be misunderstood. She is superior in every other way. This experience is also repeated with grandparents — not so often, but with even more serious results because they 'suspect' and are disappointed in us and do what they can for our children to give them *some* religion."

It can be peculiarly exasperating to religious liberals, who are really working hard at a new kind of religious education, to be accused of giving our children *no* religious training, just because other people can't recognize what we are doing as religious.

We ought not to be surprised that this happens. Religious pioneers and prophets have struggled with this problem throughout the ages. Because we try to encourage in children an awareness of the life-giving experiences that are the essence of religion, going behind the words and forms that are often empty shells, we may be considered irreligious. But we should remember that the Sadducees and Pharisees in

Jesus' day were slow to see that what he was doing and teaching was really religious.

Just as *new* ways in discipline have been misunderstood to mean *no* ways of discipline, so *new* ways in religious education are easily misunderstood as *no* ways. So we should not despair. Perhaps someone will produce a manual for baby sitters, relatives, and neighbors that will present simply the new ways in religious education, just as there are pamphlets that do it for new ways in child guidance.

We should prepare ourselves to be misunderstood, not only by the groups already mentioned, but even to a certain extent by our own children. Even though they respond enthusiastically to the kind of creative religious education we provide for them at home or in the liberal church school, they too may adopt the stereotyped definition of the word "religion" that is easily absorbed in our culture.

A mother who was teaching the kindergarten in a liberal church school one Sunday came home from her duties very excited.

"We had a real religious experience at Sunday school today," she reported to the family at dinner. "We saw a Promethea moth come out of the cocoon and fly away. The children were thrilled."

"Huh," said the nine-year-old daughter of the family, rather disgusted and feeling a little superior. "What's religious about that? It didn't have anything to do with God and Jesus."

It is not always evident to our children that the vital experiences we share with them are to take the place of the religious training their friends receive in the orthodox church schools. Not until they are seven or eight years old do children give meaning to general subjects like "arithmetic," "geography," "religion." Then, to their chagrin, our children find that what their queer family calls religion no one else seems to, and what others consider religion is either ignored or regarded critically by their family.

Many of us find it difficult to explain in positive terms why the label "religious" belongs to the experiences and books that we emphasize in the religious education of our children. We may find it simpler merely to point out the errors in orthodox religious beliefs and practices. Indeed, very often all that our children can understand is that we *don't* believe what apparently everyone else *does* believe.

This was made vivid to one mother in a conversation with her eight-year-old daughter. They had been talking about important ideas in various denominations. The mother began explaining an Episcopalian belief.

"Do you believe what they believe?" asked the little girl rather hopefully, having listened to her mother discard belief after belief.

"Oh, no!" exclaimed her mother, with perhaps too much vigor.

"Golly," said the child, "don't you believe anything?"

The mother felt she had learned a lesson. It was not clear to the little girl that her mother put aside the narrower beliefs they had been discussing because of her more inclusive beliefs. The mother realized that she needed to find words and occasions to express positively what she did believe.

It is normal and healthy for our children to be curious about the religious ways of others. If we react frankly and maturely when they come to us with their questions, it is more likely that the door will remain open for communication with them in this important area.

3

The Languages of Understanding

"But, Mother, that doesn't explain the white dresses."

Many of us religious liberals have not given sufficient thought to what we believe. We recite no creed. We have no finished faith, once revealed and now neatly packaged in a book. Are we in danger then of going to the opposite extreme — of being hopelessly vague about what we believe?

Actually most religious liberals believe a great deal. We need to know what these beliefs are. Where should we begin a fresh attempt to formulate our adult convictions? The great questions about God, freedom, and immortality may have agitated us in our college years and helped bring about the downfall of our childhood faith; but they may now seem remote and irrelevant.

Earning a living, caring for our families, getting along with our children, working on home, community, and national projects — these are now our vital concerns. Perhaps we should realize that our need is not to "find something" to believe — but rather to discover what our lives indicate that we believe right now. This is the place to start.

What did we enjoy most in the day just passed? How did we spend our time? How do we wish we might have spent it? How did we feel about ourselves at the end of the day? Do we like the kind of person we are? What do we worry about? What are we afraid of? What do we hope for? Whose lives did our lives touch during the day? Was it for better or for worse? How do we feel about parents, spouse,

children, neighbors, the schools, the town? Are we aware of
the natural universe? Do the arts influence us, and feed our
spirits?

To bring our attitudes, our convictions, our practices, out
into the open and to look at them systematically is to find
out what we actually believe. For many of us it is not easy
to bring our beliefs up to the surface where we can look at
them. We may find that we need the help and the companionship of others in order to accomplish anything fruitful. Might not such a process be part of the program of
liberal churches and fellowships?

In many of the orthodox churches the minister's function
as preacher consists largely in proclaiming the truth that has
been revealed and in helping his congregation to make this
truth their own. The liberal religious minister in his preach-
ing is more likely to take us on an excursion into thought,
raising important questions and often sharing with us his
answers to these questions. But is this really our need? Is
this the most effective means of helping us to a mature religion?

It has been suggested that in the liberal churches an important function of the minister might be "facilitator of
learning," filling the Socratic role of midwife to thought.
Perhaps we need someone, trained among other things in
leading group thinking, to help us work through our insights
together — not to tell us what we *ought* to do or believe, but
to help us look squarely at what we *are* doing and what in
fact we *do* believe.

Religious liberals may have taken too intellectualized an
approach both to what constitutes religious beliefs and how
these beliefs are arrived at. We need to experiment with a
variety of ways of reaching a clarification of our religious
convictions. Goodwin Watson makes an interesting suggestion: "It might be helpful to try a kind of group therapy
approach in religious education. Within a congenial group

of adults or teen-agers, present briefly a religious symbol (perhaps a term, a phrase, an art form, or an act of ritual). Then ask each member to close his eyes, relax, and let arise whatever images or feelings are associated for him with that symbol. Try to discover the common core of response and to help each individual correct for his deviations."[1]

Are liberal ministers trained for any such approach? We need a re-evaluation of our theological education to consider such matters. To take such a suggestion seriously might mean as revolutionary an approach to the ministry to adults as has been taking place in the ministry to children in the liberal churches. We need to ask whether eleven o'clock Sunday morning is the best time for this adult education to take place. Should we not consider separating, in time and place, this function of the church, which the sermon has been supposedly performing, from what has been traditionally called the worship function of the church? Creative thinking is being done on such questions, and more needs to be done.

Using a variety of approaches, then, we should continually try to clarify our actual beliefs. At the same time we will want to work out the relationship among our own beliefs, the best thinking of other people, and the teachings of the traditional religions of the world.

Many of us may find that our own personal philosophy is quickened most by writers who do not use theological terms — novelists, playwrights, scientists. Nonetheless, it is important for us to try to relate the speculations of non-theological thinkers with that of theological thinkers of the ages. To do this will decrease our negative and defensive feelings about traditional religion and lessen our feelings of uneasiness when children come to us with their questions.

We may find that we are quite ignorant about the beliefs and practices of religious orthodoxy. Those who are rebels from orthodoxy may have forced the whole subject into their unconscious, preferring to forget all about it. But, for reasons already pointed out, this is no solution, especially for parents and teachers. This book will suggest readings that religious liberals may find helpful for information about Judeo-Christianity and other religions of the world.

We shall wish also to work out the implications of our own beliefs for the positive religious education of our children. We may be greatly helped by two books in particular: *Consider the Children: How They Grow*, by Elizabeth M. Manwell and Sophia L. Fahs,[2] and *Today's Children and Yesterday's Heritage,* by Mrs. Fahs.[3] But in the end we must do the bulk of the thinking for ourselves. Unless we do, in a generation or two the new ways in religious education will have become just as stereotyped, just as far removed from experience, as the old ways now seem.

Parents and teachers should not guide their children in a certain way in religious education simply because it is the way suggested by leaders in religious education in the various religious groups. It is far sounder to have basic thinking on such matters going on in every church, fellowship, and home, so that what is taught is what each of us personally sees is implied by his own convictions.

Walt Whitman once wrote: "I am not so anxious to give you the truth. But I am very anxious to have you understand that all truth and power are feeble to you except your own. Can I beget a child for you?"[4]

A liberal religious mother reports: "My little girl, six, is evidently making a transition in her mind from the idea of God as a sort of Santa Claus to a larger, if vaguer, conception. My own conception isn't completely determined, so how could I expect hers to be?" Do we not really believe that the process of arriving at a concept becomes part of the concept itself, and that it is therefore impossible for anyone to hand over his concepts to another person — least of all a concept of God? Even if the mother had a crystal-clear idea of God worked out for herself, she could not "give" it to her daughter.

Those holding an orthodox religious point of view take pride in handing on to their children their faith, the faith of their fathers. Religious liberals are often ridiculed for maintaining that children should make up their own minds as to what they believe. It is, of course, absurd to think that they will make up their minds in a vacuum. To say that we cannot give our religious concepts to our children does not mean that we can be of no help to them in their own religious pilgrimage. For we will, of course, start them off and guide them in a direction suggested by our religious philosophy, using the educational methods implied by it. We will go out of our way to expose them to certain kinds of stories, to stretch their minds and sympathies with certain kinds of questions. Beyond this, the beliefs and values they finally adopt will be their own. We may legitimately hope that they will arrive at concepts basically in sympathy with our own. Better still, we should hope they will be able to extend their horizons beyond the limits which parents of our generation can reach.

Having stressed the need to clarify what we believe, as one necessary prerequisite for liberal religious parents and teachers, let us turn to a related problem. How can religious liberals who know what they believe best express their most vital beliefs?

Liberal religion is often criticized for lack of warmth. What the critics refer to is not the degree of vigor with which we hold our beliefs, but the ways in which we express the real content of our position. We have emphasized rational statements as a means of expressing our beliefs. But, for a large proportion of mankind, rational formulation has not seemed to be the most important thing that they have wanted from religion; they have seemed more eager that religion warm their hearts than that it enlighten their minds.

Must we choose to express our religious beliefs either in ways that are intellectually sound or in ways that are emotionally satisfying? A good deal of traditional religion, we believe, accentuates and encourages unhealthy emotional expression among its adherents. But is it not equally unhealthy to have a religious position that provides no way for expressing, through our feelings, our grasp of the meanings in our experience?

In so far as we religious liberals have considered reasoned statements of the intellect the only legitimate way to express our understanding of life, we may have denied a real need of all mankind, robbing our religion of warmth and color.

In our religion we should be able to express our total reaction to life, both through statements that satisfy our need for a rational understanding of experience and through forms that satisfy our need for an emotional understanding of experience. We *do* understand with both minds and hearts — that is, with our entire selves. We express this understanding both in reasoned statements and in the languages of our feelings, including painting, music, sculpture, the dance, literature. If we neglect either way of expressing our understanding, we cannot be whole persons.

Rational thought has had both theoretical and practical results; the development of scientific understanding has led to increasingly efficient ways of finding shelter, clothing, and food. But the need to express meaning in emotionally satisfying forms is equally real. In no culture has man been content to live by bread alone. In every culture, primitive or complex, men not only eat but embellish their meals with ceremonials, rituals, recipes. They not only wear clothes but create costumes, masks, styles, from cloth of different patterns, colors, designs, textures. Men not only build houses but find varieties of architectural forms, and fill them with various styles of furnishings.

Nowhere in the world has man been content to walk through life; he has danced and skipped, sung and composed poetry, created myths, legends, and cosmic dramas. A religion that has no room for these fruits of the spirit is one-sided, meager, and confining. The arts are the languages of our feelings, and without them our feelings are mute. Even the unspectacular Quaker way provides a variety of forms for the expression of feeling; the silence is a ceremonial, the handshake at the close of the meeting is a ritual, the simplicity of language and dress has symbolic significance.

These languages of the emotions seem to have their own logic. To test whether these languages succeed in saying something, we should not ask: Do they make propositions that pass the test of literal truth or picture things as they prosaically are? Rather we should ask: Do they present, accurately and vividly, with color and warmth, meanings we wish to express?

An example of a logical sentence is this: A human baby must have a human father and a human mother. This statement is either true or false. But, when we want to express how we feel about the baby and the values we assign him, we use words in another way — the way words are used in a poem or a creed or a myth. Someone is described as "born of the virgin Mary," or "child of the sun," or "daughter of the moon." Here we should not ask whether the sentence or phrase is literally true. What we must ask of this kind of statement is: Does it express well the values we associate with this person?

If someone asks, "What is a skylark?" our reply will be determined by the purpose for which the person wishes an answer. If he wishes to know for scientific purposes, we will describe the bird's size, shape, color, song, all in general terms that will fit any skylark. But, if we are asked in order to give another person as nearly as possible the emotional experience of seeing and hearing a skylark, we might answer with the poet:

> Hail to thee, blithe spirit!
> Bird thou never wert.

This statement is not literally true — but what an irrelevant test to apply to a line of poetry!

We do not have to choose either one description or the other. We know that both are important, and both have their appropriate uses.

The way of poetry and the arts generally is important when we are trying to *present* experienced values, to give others the enjoyment of them. This is the way of appreciation and worship.

> When I heard the learn'd astronomer,
> When the proofs, the figures, were ranged in columns be-
>   fore me,
> When I was shown the charts and diagrams, to add, divide,
>   and measure them,
> When I sitting heard the astronomer when he lectured with
>   much applause in the lecture-room,
> How soon unaccountable I became tired and sick
> Till rising and gliding out I wandered off by myself
> In the mystical moist night-air, and from time to time,
> Looked up in perfect silence at the stars.[5]

Religious liberalism is at times as little appreciated as the learned astronomer was by the poet when he wanted to wor-ship — not analyze — the stars. If a religious service consists largely of proofs, charts, dividing and measuring, we too may find people quietly slipping out the door.

We do not believe that there is a basic contradiction be-tween a rational statement of our beliefs and an artistic ex-pression of these beliefs. But we do think there is a good historical reason for the apparent incompatibility of the two ways in modern Christianity, and for the fact that liberal religion has slighted the emotional needs of men and women. It is a result, in part, of the period of history in which we live.

The scientific world view that began to dominate men's thinking two or three hundred years ago has punctured the Christian myth. Many intelligent men and women today believe that traditional Christianity embodies inadequate natural science, anthropology, sociology, psychology, and ethics. Such questioning of the prevailing myth has happened in other cultures.[6]

In the Greek culture, Plato brought his rational intellect to bear on the myths that expressed the religion of his contemporaries. He found not only that the myths were not literally true, but that they taught an inadequate natural science and poor ethics; he therefore questioned their value for the young. He did this at a time when the sun of the Greek gods was setting; his criticism was a symptom of the times. Thought had become so systematized that it was able to analyze and dissect the old myths.

This is the stage we have reached in relation to Christianity. The fact that people argue about its literal truth or falsity indicates that our thinking and feeling have outgrown this old way of trying to understand life.[7] The orthodox who claim that all parts of the old Christian story of salvation are literally true, the liberal rationalists who argue that it is all literally false — both are equally in error. The wrong test is being applied. It is irrelevant to bring the test of literal truth to it at all. Our quarrel with it must be on the grounds that it is not an adequate vehicle for our thought or feelings.[8]

We can no longer see the world in the same way as those who drew up the large outlines of this myth. We have too many basic disagreements with its underlying pre-scientific concepts. Probably the majority of persons drawn to liberal religion enjoy systematic thinking and cannot be satisfied with a religion that is expressed in ways out of harmony with their keenest thoughts. The poetry, the theology (which is probably a form of poetry), the art generally of Christian orthodoxy — these do not fit the thinking and feeling of many of us.

Walt Whitman expressed the problem over a hundred years ago. "What a comment it forms, anyhow . . . with the splendid day-rise of science and resuscitation of history, that our chief religious and political works are not our own, nor adapted to our light, but have been furnished by far-back ages out of their arriere and darkness, or, at most, twilight dimness!"[9]

Yet the Christian myth has been the vision that filled men's eyes for centuries. Not only has it provided the large ideas that Western thinking has worked with and worked over, but it has also shaped men's feelings, so that our major works of art have expressed this myth. When the religious liberal reluctantly but decisively discards the myth, he must to some extent also discard the rich fruits of other men's artistic creations based on this myth.

And so the religious liberal appears to be left with a vacuum for his feelings. He lacks an emotional vision of the meaning of life, and he lacks the ability to enjoy other men's creative expressions of their feelings about this vision.

But in fact there are at least three ways open for the religious liberal to express with his feelings his understanding of life.

First, we can each be a creative artist. We can lead lives close to nature and live with deep and varied human contacts. In so far as we wish to share our experienced values with others, we must express these through whatever creative art we are masters of. Our churches might well be centers of experimentation in this field. The sharing of immediately felt values is what Walt Whitman tried to achieve in *Leaves of Grass:* "*Leaves of Grass* indeed . . . has mainly been the

outcropping of my own emotional and other personal nature
— an attempt, from first to last, to put a *Person*, a human being (myself, in the latter half of the nineteenth century, in
America) freely, fully and truly on record." [10]

The great religions of the world have often celebrated the
lives of persons who themselves had no desire to be celebrated, but who, because they lived such vital lives, caught
men's poetic imagination. What many of the great figures of
religion yearned for was that everyone should live as close
to reality as they did. The irony of history is the misuse that
has been made of the lives and insights of these creative religious men. Ideally, liberal religion urges every man to put
himself "on record."

A second course for us religious liberals is to turn to the
secular arts to find already created forms for our feelings.
Susanne Langer writes:

> When the arts have become "liberated," as the saying is, from re-
> ligion, they simply have exhausted the religious consciousness, and
> draw upon other sources. . . . Then the most impressive, living art
> leaves the religious context, and draws on unrestricted feeling some-
> where else. It cannot do otherwise, but in so doing it loses its tradi-
> tional sphere of influence, the solemn, festive populace, and runs the
> danger of never reaching beyond the studio where it was created.[11]

The liberal churches should take up this art and celebrate
it. A great deal of contemporary art would express adequately our feelings about experience. Some ministers are
already experimenting in this direction, finding, for example,
in great lyric poetry much material that is appropriate for
new song books in our churches.[12]

And, finally, there is a third possibility: the religious liberal can experiment with great art from the various orthodox
religions of the world. If no one orthodoxy can claim our
complete allegiance, several placed side by side may serve
us as vehicles of truth. Poetry, sculpture, music, philosophy,
the dance, produced by artists of various religions and then

brought together, might create forms for our feelings. Here, too, liberal religious leaders are experimenting.

It is important, then, that we religious liberals find and create adequate forms for the artistic expression of our most vital beliefs. We must do this both for our own emotional satisfaction and in order that our children, as they grow, will not feel as bereft in this area as many religious liberals in the last generation or two have felt.

Actually, of course, one of the finest things about our new ways in religious education is that it encourages children to live richly. We want them to live deeply in the here-and-now, and to express with their minds and through creative activities their reactions to experience. Perhaps not until a generation or two of these children have grown up will we begin to have adequate forms for our adult liberal religious feelings.

If our analysis in this chapter is pointing in the right direction, it may give us some theoretical understanding of something that has puzzled a good many of us.

One troubled mother reports: "Many of the dogmatic beliefs make no sense to our child. When we explain the beliefs, he not only cannot believe them, but cannot see how anyone can." This mother is rightly concerned. She realizes that an explanation that, when it is finished, leaves just as much to be explained is inadequate.

In so far as we have tended to treat religious ideas and practices as if they only represented men's rational understanding, our religious explanations have, in the end, often proved to be no explanations at all.

Another liberal religious mother was attempting to explain First Communion to her nine-year-old daughter. She related it, as simply as she could, to the last supper Jesus ate with his disciples. She explained that people have had different understandings of what Jesus said and what Jesus meant on that occasion.

"But, Mother," said the little girl, remembering her friends' preparation for communion, "that doesn't explain the white dresses."

How right she was! The fact is that many of our rationalistic explanations sound irrelevant — not only to the orthodox but also to our children. We may prove to our satisfaction that certain items in creeds or myths are literally false, while we fail utterly to account for their appeal to so many people, past and present. If we really hope to interpret traditional religion helpfully to our children, we must give them a convincing explanation for the tremendous role that creeds, rituals, and traditional dogmas have played in religion. This is possible if we can show that these "unbelievable" dogmas and apparently impractical rituals are ways people have of expressing their beliefs through their feelings. When people are doing this, they use words differently than when they are making statements of fact.

We must help our children to try to visualize the world in the terms of those who developed the various parts of the Christian myth. Our children should realize that we cannot go back in our own thinking and feeling to these pre-scientific ways; it is out of the question for us to *believe* these things. But our children can be helped to feel themselves into this thought world for the purpose of attempting to understand it.

With such an approach as this, our children will be less likely to scoff at unbelievable dogmas, less likely to be at a loss to understand how anyone could take such beliefs seriously. They will see that they should not ask about religious beliefs and practices: Are they literally true or false? Do they really work? They should ask: How did those who thought and acted in these ways think and feel about life?

What mental and emotional contradictions are there for those who today are trying to live in both of these thought worlds at the same time?

Perhaps we liberal religious parents have been a little afraid to give adequate explanations of dogmas and practices, for fear that our explanations might make the positions too attractive to our children. Knowing that the "white dresses" seem desirable to our little girls, we may say to ourselves, "Well, at least we aren't going to make them *logical.*"

Often, therefore, we have been less able to give our children a sympathetic picture of orthodox Judeo-Christianity than of contemporary Buddhism and Hinduism, the religion of the Eskimo and American Indian, even the religion of prehistoric man. The beliefs and practices of these groups are no more logical than those of orthodox Christianity, but at least we have not feared that our child might "become one." We have felt freer to make vivid the thought world and feeling world of orthodoxies of the far away or long ago than those of contemporary Christian orthodoxy.

Liberal religious parents, teachers, and ministers have no easy task as they attempt to interpret traditional religion to children. We need to do much more thinking about the complementary roles of reason and the emotions in religious thought and practice. As we become more secure in our positive beliefs, as we develop richer modes for their expression, we will feel freer and more competent in our roles as interpreters.

so. A dogmatic defense is the only possible defense for truths given dogmatically, without any background for understanding them.

After one mother had listened to a very heated theological argument among four- and five-year-olds, she wrote: "I was impressed by the angry flare-ups between the two children who had been indoctrinated equally, but differently."

A child who has been given dogmatic teachings and has been told explicitly or has understood implicitly that these dogmas are *the* true ones will feel threatened by the fact that people don't all agree with Mother and Daddy. Children who have been taught to expect difference of opinion should increasingly feel the experience of it as reassuring, not threatening.

Differences in religious viewpoints become very real to four- and five-year-olds when they discover that their family goes to the church on Main Street while their friends, who in every other way seem very much like them, go to church on Maple Street. Why? The theoretical reasons for denominational differences are, of course, far beyond the grasp of such young children. Can this fact of their experience be handled helpfully on a very simple level?

In the "Martin and Judy" books there is a story called "Children's Day at the Church."[1] In this story Martin wonders why his family goes to the church so far from home instead of the one right down the street. His father explains that different churches exist because people like to think about God in different ways, and that when Martin is old enough to understand the differences he may go where he wishes. This would seem to be an adequate treatment of this matter for young children.

But, by the age of six or seven and even with some mature five-year-olds, it is not satisfying to learn simply that different fathers and mothers and churches teach different

things. A new need begins to assert itself — the need to begin to gain some understanding of why these matters are
something about which people differ so drastically. After all,
some people don't teach that two and two are four, and
others that two and two are five; why do people teach such
different things about God and Jesus?

Six-year-old Teddy came home from playing with some
friends.

"Is Jesus magic?" he asked.

"No," answered Mother, "Jesus isn't magic, but many
people think he could perform miracles. We believe he was
a fine man and a great leader."

"Well, then, why do Bill and Tommy believe Jesus is
magic? Why do they tell them he is at Bible school?"

Why *do* adults teach things that children interpret to mean
that Jesus was magic? How can we best answer this kind of
query?

Charlie, seven years old, was playing on the backyard
swing with his friend Robert. Charlie's parents were religious
liberals, and there was no liberal church in town.

"You'll go to Hell if you don't go to church every Sunday," said Robert.

Charlie jumped off the swing and went to find his mother.
"Is it true you'll go to Hell if you don't go to church every
Sunday? Robert says you will."

"Well," said Mother, "some people believe in Hell and the
Devil, the way people used to believe in witches."

"But there aren't any real witches, Mother, are there?"
asked Charlie.

"No, there aren't," said Mother.

"Is there a real Devil?"

"No," said Mother.

"Then why does Robert say there is and that there's a
Hell?"

"Because it is what he believes," said Mother.

This mother reports: "I think my boy was *not* satisfied. He wanted some sort of concrete proof one way or the other. He wanted to believe what I told him, but Robert's positive attitude still disturbed him."

She was quite right in saying that it was not satisfying to Charlie to be told simply, "It is what he believes." Actually, it would have been closer to the truth to say, "This is what Robert has been taught." But this still leaves the question: "Why has Robert been taught this?" To end the discussion here suggests that the liberal religious parents don't know or understand about these matters either, and that, for all they know, Robert and his family may be right.

These conversations indicate that even as young as six our children need help in beginning to understand that people talk not only literally but also in poetry. For Teddy's mother to say only that Jesus was a fine man and a great leader throws no light for Teddy on the here-and-now fact that a great many people believe that Jesus was a doer of magic or miracles. She could, to help him here, say that people made up wonder stories about Jesus, just as they have about other heroes — like Davy Crockett or Johnny Appleseed. It is a way people have of expressing their feelings about great men.

And Charlie's mother could be frank and direct about her own disbelief in a literal Hell and Devil. She could then relate these ideas to old stories that people made up long ago to try to help them understand about their world. Our children need to grasp the fact that myth and legend and epic poetry are fruits of one way that the mind of man has grappled with experience. They will study about these things when they are a little older.

But we must be careful here, in meeting this need to understand man's myth-making tendencies, that we do not confuse and even frighten children. For many years still these children will be grappling with the distinction between what is real and possible and what is make-believe and impossible. And they still are equipped with a very primitive sense of time and space, so that long-ago and far-away events are not yet seen in proper perspective.

Moreover, studies in child development suggest that in these early years excessive worry and guilt feelings all too easily develop. Children are growing out of the "cute" age, and may be in the process of being "brought to heel." Discipline may be suddenly enforced by threat and the actual carrying out of punishments of various kinds.

Parents and church-school workers report a great fascination among children of about five to eight with talk about the Devil, and burning up in Hell, and God's punishing people. These adults report fears of God's magic powers and His all-seeing eye. Confused by what their friends say has literally happened and will happen to bad people, confused further by television and comic books as to what evil forces actually exist and could reach them, fed by their own real tensions and worries, the children are further confused by some of the frightening dogmas of traditional religion. Such teachings contribute to the burden of worries that these young children already carry around with them.

Children's excessive talk of Hell and the Devil and God's punishment of evildoers may reflect their own real fear of parents and teachers, and worry about what grownups may do to them. If children persist in talking about these matters, we parents and teachers will do well to listen with "the third ear" and try to relate what is said to any real worries and fears that we may suspect our children have. Positively, we will want to reduce tension in all the ways we can and, at the same time, very matter-of-factly reject the literal truth of the dogmas with which the children may be frightening themselves.

A mother reports: "Nancy, who is five, has recently been wetting her pants a good deal. She asked me if I thought that God could see everything she did, and could He see when her pants were wet? I told her I did not think of God in that way, as a person who sees everyone, and then I proceeded to search my mind for factors that could be contributing to increased tension in Nancy's small world."

The story of the baby Moses and the killing of all the other boy babies, so long a favorite in church nurseries and kindergartens, has fostered children's real fears and guilt feelings. With no grasp of long ago and far away, these little children may wonder if their own baby brothers and sisters are next on the list.

Four-year-old Jane went on a week-end visit to see her grandmother. She attended Sunday school at her grandmother's church. There Jane listened with much interest to the story of the baby Moses. She had never heard it before; it was fascinating and important to her. Jane had a new baby sister.

Jane's mother reports: "That night Jane dreamed a wicked king killed her new sister, of whom she was, of course, jealous. She wanted reassurance that this could not actually happen (even though she might want it to) and wanted to know how we felt about the story. The dream was repeated several times."

Many children have been frightened and upset when told the story of Herod's threat at the time of the birth of Jesus.

Another old nursery favorite, Noah and his ark, has also been known to stimulate fear. One six-year-old girl listened to a vivid retelling of this story in an orthodox Sunday school. The teacher said that the story tells how God loved and took care of Noah because he was a good man. But this was not at all what the story meant to this particular six-year-old listener. It fitted right into her very real worries and fears. Perhaps it did tell of Noah who had been good and was saved, but it also told of the rest of mankind who had been evil and were drowned as a punishment by God. The teacher reported that later in the week during a thunderstorm this child became hysterical. She was sure God would drown her because she hadn't been good.[2]

The fact that these old stories often function in this way is not surprising. They developed in a thought world in which it was believed that children were naturally evil and needed to be frightened into goodness.

Those who are tempted to tell their children the great old stories of our culture just to make them Biblically literate might ponder such incidents. Is not our greatest obligation to the youngest children to minister to their vital developmental needs, rather than to thrust our cultural heritage upon them at as young an age as possible?

5

The Older Child and His Questions

"I just wish we were more like other people."

When children first enter school they become more acutely aware that people differ about religious matters. They discover that there are groups representing these differences — groups to which most of them belong, whether they like it or not. Unfortunately this is just the age when children are beginning to feel a need to club together, and they discover themselves to be parts of religious units that divide up their natural groups. The adult controversies that created the groups are not appropriate study for children in the elementary grades, and yet the fact of their existence first confronts children in the early years of school.

The various groups are not at all clearly defined in the children's minds.

"There are fifteen first communions in my class," announced David one day, fresh home from the first grade.

"And what are they?" asked his mother, her curiosity aroused as to what "first communions" meant to her son when used in this way.

"Well, they usually wear crosses," he said, "and they're usually Catholics."

It is difficult, before eight or nine, for children even to grasp the division of the three large groups in our country, Roman Catholic, Protestant, and Jewish. And it is even more difficult for them to realize that denominational names like Congregational, Episcopalian, Methodist, all fall under one large heading, Protestant. (They have the same kind of difficulty trying to understand that names of cities fall under the larger heading, state.) One effect of this is for Protestant children in some parts of our country to tend to envy their Roman Catholic friends, who are in so overwhelming a majority.

Just as soon as we feel that the information is at all understandable, we will want to give our children the simplest facts behind the major religious divisions in our culture. But in fact amazingly little of this material is comprehensible to children under ten. One book that is a helpful source for this information is *One God: The Ways We Worship Him.*[1] The text can be used with ten-year-olds, and the fine pictures make the distinctive characteristics of the three major groups vividly real. However, the book is written from a traditional point of view, and calls for some interpretation by liberal religious parents; Protestantism is presented as chiefly trinitarian. Another valuable source book for parents seeking information about various Protestant denominations is *The Church Across the Street;* it also contains chapters on the history, beliefs, and practices of Judaism and Catholicism.[2] The discussions in this book have been checked for accuracy by representatives of the various groups.

But the really important problem for these youngsters is how to satisfy their emotional need to identify with their friends. Such identification is thwarted by religious differences. And the children of religious liberals make the even more disturbing discovery that somehow their family is even "more different" than most families.

For children in this age group, it is more desirable to agree with their friends than with their parents. They feel almost no need to hold the "right" theological position, since in most cases the ideas that make up the theological position are far beyond their understanding.

One mother reports: "Every time I try to discuss the anthropomorphic ideas of God that our six-year-old daughter brings home from her friends and start my discussion with, 'Some people think as your friend does,' she firmly interrupts with, 'And *I am one* of them!'" It does not seem to be too important to the children what brand of blue jeans they wear, what breakfast cereal they eat, what television show they watch, or what church they go to — as long as it is the same one as that of the majority of their friends. A frequently reported remark is: "I don't care what they believe; why can't we all go to the same church?"

It seems, in the light of our present limited knowledge, that the pressure children feel to conform to the ways of the majority varies at different points in their development. We need to be sensitive to the times when they feel it most strongly.

Listen to this rather wistful conversation between a mother and her twelve-year-old son, Gil, and ten-year-old daughter, Frances.

"Oh, Mama," said Frances. "I just wish we were more like other people!"

"Why, Honey," exclaimed Mother, "what do you mean?"

"Oh, that we could just go to the regular old churches and believe God makes you good, and that if you believe all that about Jesus, you'll go to Heaven — and let it go at that!"

"But — but, dear —," stammered Mother.

"Yes," broke in Gil, "but Frances, then you have to believe you might go to Hell. And that scares me!"

Mother began fumbling for words. "One's religious beliefs," she said, "evolve slowly and include . . ."

"I know, I know," said Frances, with some impatience. "But the other kids don't worry about war, or Negroes, or how they feel about anything. They just learn Bible verses!"

"I agree with Frances," said Gil emphatically. "It would be a lot easier if we could just say, 'We're Baptists,' and then believe whatever you're supposed to believe to go to Heaven. But it's too late now. We've already thought too much about it!"

One is reminded of the lines in *The Brothers Karamazov*, "I tell thee that man is tormented by no greater anxiety than to find someone quickly to whom he can hand over that gift of freedom with which the ill-fated creature is born."[3] We parents have chosen to try to keep the burden of freedom on our children's shoulders; but at the same time we must be alert to the developmental needs of our children.

The specific events or circumstances that will cause the children of religious liberals to feel their being different most keenly — these will vary from situation to situation.

One parent reports that for her the difficulty has centered around the occurrence of released time for religious-education classes and summer Bible school. For several years, her daughter Marjorie, now seven, was urged by her best friend, Nancy, to attend weekday Bible classes and vacation Bible school. Attendance meant extra treats, movies, and a radio appearance. The two little girls were close friends, and Nancy's mother was one of the teachers. Usually, as the weekly discussion came up, in spite of every effort, tears and temper tantrums occurred.

One day Marjorie said crossly, "Why *can't* I go? Don't we believe in God and Jesus?"

"Well," replied her mother, "we believe in God, but we think different things about Him than Nancy's family do. We believe that Jesus was a great teacher and we try to follow the things he taught."

"Well then, why *can't* I go?" insisted Marjorie angrily.

"Because," said the mother in desperation, "we're Universalists and not Baptists. You must make up your mind. If you would rather be a Baptist, be one. You can't be both. The ways of teaching are entirely different, and it is too confusing to go to both. So, if you insist on going with Nancy, then you will have to be a Baptist and stop going to the Universalist church with us."

The mother comments: "I was disturbed at having to put such a choice up to a six-year-old and if I could find a better way of accomplishing the same result, I'd use it. She chose 'to be a Universalist,' but I'm afraid her decision was based on fear of being rejected by her family and not on *real religious conviction*."

Of course we must agree with the mother that the decision was not based on "real religious conviction." At six Marjorie could have no grasp of the issues separating the two denominations; for her all that separated them was a couple of streets. The real choice for Marjorie lay between her friends and her family, and she reluctantly chose her family. Perhaps if the mother had felt less on the defensive she could have handled the situation in a less upsetting manner.

It is more realistic to speak of what "mother and father believe" than of what "we believe," since beliefs are not something transmitted automatically like a family name. It might have been more helpful to Marjorie to suggest, as in the "Martin and Judy" story cited earlier, that the choice of a church hinges on an understanding of questions she is as yet too young to explore, but will want to study when she is old enough. One might also suggest to such a child that she is studying now the kinds of things that will make her able to make an intelligent choice of a church when she is older.

Sometimes it is helpful in such a situation to point out that parents differ about many things beside religion. Not all parents agree about what television shows they allow their children to watch; what, if any, comic books they welcome into the home; what hours they expect children to go to bed.

These differences are the outcome of beliefs and convictions that adults have, and need to have, to be good parents.

Children respect parents who have an intelligent concern for them, especially if they are able to talk it over openly and not defensively.

Katherine Wensberg's story "Families Are Different" is helpful as a starter for a parent-child discussion in this kind of situation.[4]

Two other books that are useful in a more general way are *All About Us*, by Eva Knox Evans,[5] and *The Story of People* by May Edel.[6] These books can help children and parents discuss together the whole idea that people can differ from each other in many important ways and yet live happily together.

Children may be helped to accept the differences that are related to religious ideas by hearing the familiar story, "The Blind Men and the Elephant." This can be found in Sophia Fah's excellent collection, *From Long Ago and Many Lands*.[7] In this story Buddha quiets his disputing disciples by showing them that they are as foolish to quarrel about their partial insights on ultimate questions as the blind men who quarreled over what an elephant was like. A seven-year-old will not spontaneously see the analogy between religious questions and what an elephant is; but a nine-year-old quickly grasps that we are all as blind men about these questions.

Some liberal religious parents are tempted just to let their children go along with their friends to the traditional church groups and hope for the best. Others feel that this tends to make our liberalism appear too careless and haphazard, and to give tacit approval to what is orthodox teaching. The Universalist mother quoted earlier did not follow this path because, she reports: "An older daughter, at the age of six, attended an orthodox Bible school where she was taught the evils of the world in general; and it took years to undo the damage. I did not wish to repeat the experience."

On the other hand, there may well be situations where for a particular child at a particular point in his development, when all the values are weighed, it is better to let him go along with the majority group. Each of us must help our children to meet this problem in the best way that we can. (Of course, it is something quite different when a child wants to visit a friend's church just to satisfy his curiosity. We feel that such an excursion will be most fruitful if the liberal parent goes along too, and afterwards interprets the experience.)

If we find our children continually pleading to go along with their friends, it might be a good idea to evaluate what we are doing positively for our children. If we liberal parents are willing to go a little farther than the majority of parents, we can probably minister to the social needs of children without sacrificing our basic viewpoint and values.

Indeed, simply to welcome children into the backyard, or into the house itself, has value. It is astonishing the number of homes in which the door, from morning until supper time, is shut to all children, even those who live there. Paint and clay and records and games available and free to be used — these mark a home as one in which someone cares about children and what they are interested in.

Besides this we should arrange extra group experiences of significance for children. There is no need to find a group of children of liberal religious families, for by giving children from homes with a variety of viewpoints an opportunity to share important experiences, we can demonstrate our liberal faith. We believe that the basic experiences of life tie us together rather than separate us. These basic social experiences *are* religious experiences. We can teach religion with a backyard blue-printing group, a neighborhood star-gaze, a nature scavenger hunt, a group reading of a great book, a dramatization of a story, a neighborhood kite-flying, a bird walk, a hike, a skating party. Such experiences shared with friends whose parents teach them different words about religion can give children the real experience of what we believe, that "all men are brothers under the sun."

This is what we want our children to know, and what their drive to identify with their friends points towards. It is sad that our religious organizations destroy this natural push toward unity.

Our children not only feel a pressure to be like the majority but are soon aware that the majority position has the approval of the community. They experience the larger community through their schools; and, with rare exceptions, the public schools give sanction to traditional ways in religion. Usually, for the first few years of school, our children equate what the school authorities favor, and what their friends favor, with what is right. This puts our position in an unfavorable light. Everyone else knows the Lord's Prayer and the Twenty-third Psalm. The children of liberal parents feel they must, too; and they may care as little as the others what these things mean.

In addition, little girls, especially, will identify with a beloved teacher. They will want to like everything about her, including her religious ideas.

A second-grader from a liberal religious family came home near Christmastime very much upset by the religious ideas of her teacher. Since they were ideas about the miraculous birth of Jesus, and the child knew the facts about human birth, she could not accept what her teacher taught.

"I don't care so much how the other children believe, but why can't my teacher believe the way I do? I wish she did, so much!"

This particular little girl seemed to feel sympathetically toward her parents' point of view, but she felt and expressed clearly her very real need to admire her teacher wholeheartedly.

Such experiences are often upsetting to sensitive children. Another mother tells of the difficult situation in which she found herself when her daughter came home from the fourth grade and reported that the teacher had said, "There may be three so-called religions in the United States, Catholic, Protestant, and Jewish, but there is only one real religion and that is the Catholic."

Of course, there are many teachers with traditional beliefs who are careful to respect our American heritage of freedom of religion. But we may expect more problems of this type with the increased pressure on our schools to teach *about* religion and to emphasize moral and spiritual values.

One father reports: "Our city has a new 'moral and ethical' curriculum, leaving the decision pretty much up to the teacher on 'how' and 'what.' Our son, who is nine, came home very much disturbed by what his teacher had taught. It was very orthodox and in basic conflict with our teaching here at home and in our liberal church school. It is wrong to put a child in conflict with a teacher in an area so charged with emotion. Our son feels caught — and resents the fact that he cannot argue back."

In situations where children encounter intolerant teachers, the story "People Are Different" in *The Tuckers*[8] is quite helpful. In this story, the seven-year-old boy has a substitute teacher who, because of a lack of a sympathetic and understanding approach, gives the boy a hard day. Finally his mother and father are able to help him talk about his upsetting day at school. Mother tells him that, when a person bothers him as much as his teacher did that day, he should just remember that "people are different."

We can also tell our children that in our country the rule has been made that religion should not be taught in the public schools. Since people cannot agree about religious ideas, it has been felt that we will have a stronger and happier country if religion is taught at home and in the churches. We can tell our children that we think this is a good rule and we will do all that we can to see that it is kept.

It is interesting to look at this from the teacher's point of view, too. A religious liberal, a third-grade teacher, writes about her own way of handling religious differences when they assert themselves in her class:

"We were talking about spring. One child said God made the flowers bloom, and another said that it was not God, but nature. I said, 'In our country we want people to be free to believe what seems to them to be true, and that seems to be the best way to have it in our room here at school. Sometimes it is hard to know who is right and who is wrong. Most of the people thought Columbus was wrong in what he believed, but now the whole world knows the world is round and that Columbus was right.

" 'It is good to be with people who let you think for yourself, and believe what you think is true as long as you don't harm anyone. Most people, when they are children, think pretty much what their fathers and mothers do, but as they grow up they decide more and more for themselves what they believe. All of you might change your mind about many things when you get a little older. And that is the way it should be.' "

The teacher goes on to comment: "I think I would be matter-of-fact and use the same general approach always, varying the illustration and the length of discussion according to the age and receptivity of the children involved. This general approach seems to satisfy the children in all controversial issues — sex, politics, labor issues, Santa Claus, and the Easter Bunny."

We can hope our children will have experiences with such a teacher as this. But when they don't we can adapt this kind of conversation to our own handling of the situation.

Although our children's need to identify with their friends

and the larger community is real and pressing, they also feel a real need to test what they hear and observe about religion with their developing intellect and widening sympathies. This testing will be a process that continues all through their growing years.

A father writes: "One thing that has stood out in all these and other discussions of religious topics is the real and genuine curiosity and interest of the children from the free tradition when confronted with dogmatic beliefs."

One day six-year-old Harry reported to his mother, "Miss Vernon says that bad people get sent to Hell and are burned."

"Yes," said his mother, "lots of people believe there is a Hell. Miss Vernon is one of the people who believes that."

"Well, I don't believe it," said Harry.

"Can you tell me why you don't?" asked his mother.

"I don't think anybody would do a thing like that — burn up people."

"It seems to me to be cruel, too," said his mother.

"It's too mean," said Harry, with some relief.

Although when Harry is older he may have experiences that would make Hell a more plausible belief, at six he rejects it, because it doesn't fit in with his experiences of life. We should encourage this testing of what children hear by their own developing minds and sense of values.

One Friday eight-year-old Ruth had a classmate, Nancy, home for lunch.

"I can't eat hamburg," said Nancy.

"Why not?" said Ruth.

"Because it's against my religion."

"Why?" persisted Ruth.

"I don't know," said Nancy; "we just can't."

Later Ruth said to her mother, "Boy! I'd want to know *why* I couldn't eat meat. I wouldn't just not eat it."

We may want our children to develop an appreciation of other religious groups, but we also want them to have a healthy respect for a thoughtful approach to religion.

Children will come gradually to realize that religion has to do with inner convictions. These convictions should make an impact on our living. Beliefs that have no visible effect on how we live hardly seem important. Children want a religion that matters. Sometimes Roman Catholic orthodoxy seems to have a strategic advantage with children; the religion of the Catholic friend can be seen to affect behavior so clearly. Children are relieved to see something specific and tangible in an area that so easily appears vague and foggy to them. They may respond to the idea of definite rules about confession, church attendance, sins, fasts, and feasts. "Giving up" at Lent, memorizing the catechism, set prayers to be learned, gestures such as crossing one's self — all these make it seem that the orthodox friends *believe* so much.

One mother gives the following account of how she handled a situation in which she was able to help her child see that being religious is not something external, and that just to do something that is labeled religious is no final test of conduct.

This mother took a group of ten boys and girls, between seven and fourteen, on a hike. First they had to ride a short distance on the train. She explained to each child how much money to bring, and that those under twelve would pay half-fare. It was a school holiday, a Friday. Each child had a picnic lunch, and the mother had brought hot dogs for roasting. After the long hike they arrived at the picnic spot hungry and ready to eat. As the roasting commenced, one of the biggest boys, thirteen, announced that he couldn't eat hot dogs, since it was Friday and he was a Catholic.

The other youngsters looked rather awed. They knew how hungry everyone was, and yet this big boy was going to go without hot dogs because of his religion. It made quite an impression.

On the train ride home they all bought tickets from the conductor. The thirteen-year-old Catholic boy gave the conductor the half-fare amount. The conductor took the money and didn't question him. After the conductor had gone, the boy took great pride in the fact that he had gotten away with paying only half.

The mother who had taken the group on the hike noticed that her eight-year-old daughter was quietly observing all this, as she had his earlier refusal of a hot dog because of his religion.

That night the little girl's mother asked her why she thought George had refused the hot dog.

"Because he's a Catholic," said the little girl. "It's his religion."

"You know," said Mother, "Jesus is believed to have died on a Friday. In the Catholic Church they try to remember this by going without meat on Friday. That is supposed to help Catholics remember how Jesus was willing to die for ideas that were important to him."

Quite spontaneously the little girl said, "George shouldn't lie about not being twelve yet, should he?"

"No," said her mother, "and that's just what I was thinking about. Do you think Jesus was the kind of person who cared whether you ate hot dogs — or whether you could be depended on?"

"Depended on," said the little girl.

"One of Jesus' most famous teachings," said Mother, "was that it isn't what goes into you — what you eat or drink — that shows what kind of person you are, but what comes out of you — your ideas and feelings and actions. I think Jesus was the kind of person who would rather that George had eaten the hot dog and paid his full fare."

We have suggested that adult religious liberals need a religion that is not only intellectually sound but also emotionally satisfying. This is true for our children also. They need esthetically pleasing ways of expressing their understanding and beliefs.

One frank eight-year-old said, "I think I'd like to go to the Catholic church until I got tired of seeing all the pretty things. Then I'd tell them that I really didn't believe all those things." Actually our children *think* they are missing out more than they really are, because they adopt the narrow definition of what constitutes religion.

Have we no "pretty things" that go with our beliefs? Of course we do! We have the riches of the whole universe to draw on. We may ask ourselves: are we giving our children opportunity enough to satisfy their love of beauty and desire to surround themselves with emotionally satisfying tangible things? We can learn from children what the natural treasures of childhood are.

One mother listed what she found one morning on the bedside table of her nine-year-old daughter and on the bureau of her seven-year-old son. On the daughter's table were: one handkerchief from Japan, two Chinese cards, four pieces of broken glass of assorted colors, three ribbons, two pieces of mica, one piece of quartz, and part of a butterfly wing found on a sidewalk. On the boy's bureau were four spark plugs, three horse chestnuts, one transparent chrysalis case of a departed monarch butterfly, one sand dollar, one silver dollar, two metal springs, a cork, and a baseball card.

The mother had intended to shout out orders to "clear off the trash." But she didn't when she looked more closely — every item a treasure! It may seem like an odd assortment out of which to create a "worship" center, but that is precisely the function it served.

If we are imaginative and creative with our children, their envy of the externals of orthodoxy will not go deep. Much of the art and poetry used in orthodoxy is shoddy. We should gather and share with our children poetry, pictures, sculpture, music of the finest quality that express for every age level an esthetic grasp of reality. A member of any church may have a lovely picture of a mother by one's bed, or may sit silent in the glow of candlelight. No church has a monopoly on the symbolism inherent in light, fire, birth, growth, death. We must celebrate life and clothe it in forms that stir the minds and hearts of children.

Liberal religious parents and teachers are eager to meet all the needs of growing children. The task is not easy. Our children want warm relations with their peers, and that is good. It is a tragedy that our religions divide us instead of bind us into one family of man. We must help our children satisfy this need, and on the deepest levels of experience liberal religion can do this. It can also meet their need for an intellectually sound and emotionally satisfying religion.

6

What Kind of Answers?

*"This is my third child, and I don't seem to be getting
any better at this."*

The questions that our children ask about traditional religion are not the kind that are asked and then answered
once and for all. They are questions that the children will
ask again and again at various points in their growing up.

One mother writes: "My tendency is to be disturbed and
puzzled by these questions. My saying that I don't know of
any definite answers to some of the questions may stimulate
more questions, but it doesn't bring satisfaction to the child.
This is my third child, and I don't seem to get any better at
this with practice."

How can we best proceed so that a feeling of satisfaction
will most often be the outcome? We do not have to give
children neat answers, but we should feel when the conversation is over that we have really communicated with them
and that out of this communication has come increased insight for them. If we greet their questions with warmth and
interest, they will sense that we too have asked questions
such as these and that they are worth thinking about.

Sometimes we may have to suggest to our children that
they have gotten hold of words or ideas that are too complex
for them to handle for the time being; much as we might like
to make everything clear to them, there are some things that
just have to wait for an explanation until the children have
had more experience.

"What is adultery, Mother?" asked six-year-old Marjorie.

"Susie says it's awful and it's a sin." Susie had been learning the Ten Commandments.

Marjorie had been told how babies were born, but like most six-year-olds she had shown no interest in how the baby gets started inside the mother's body. This is not recognized by children as needing an explanation much before seven or eight. So Marjorie's mother did not see how she could possibly explain adultery, which involves an awareness of even more complex human relations.

"Susie was hearing about feelings that grown-up men and women have about each other," said Marjorie's mother. "You really can't get that word straight until you're bigger. I think that's about a nine-year-old question. Or maybe it's even a twelve-year-old question — I really don't know. But let's wait and try answering it in a few years."

If we are frank and straightforward when children ask about either complex adult concepts or complex historical material, they can accept this kind of answer. Of course, if we are just hedging or trying to put them off, they will sense that; but it seems to us legitimate, occasionally, simply to say that for the time being the question is unanswerable.

We will be more convincing if we can give our children one or two examples from their own experience of what we mean by words that can't be explained. If, when they were only two years old, they wanted to know, "Is this tomorrow?" we couldn't explain to them the kind of word "tomorrow" was until their experience had caught up with their vocabulary. Perhaps when they were three years old, we told them that we had bought Daddy a new necktie for Christmas, and we explained it was a secret. But they ran to Daddy and told him that we had a *secret* necktie for him for Christmas. They just couldn't grasp the meanings that were hidden in the word "secret" when they were three years old. Some of the ideas and words that children bring to us about religion are these kinds of words.

We can comfort ourselves by remembering that it is not only in the area of religion that children try unsuccessfully to put on words and ideas that are too grown-up. Many parents become acutely aware of the similarity between religion and politics on this score, particularly during a Presidential election. Children hear much that they sense has great emotional importance to grownups; yet most of it must remain meaningless until their own experience fills in the meaning. Attempting to "explain" a political cartoon or a joke in the *New Yorker* to a child impresses one vividly with how much experience is summed up in word symbols and picture symbols.

Admitting, then, that there are times when even the most interested, sympathetic, and informed parent or teacher must remain dumb, what of the times when an answer is called for? In the first place, we must be sure just what the question means to the particular child. The meaning of a question is a complex thing, determined in part by the person who asks it, in part by the situation that awakens it, and in part by what we might call its objective content.

We should therefore move slowly when our children come to us with their questions. Instead of rushing right into an "answer," we might say, "That's a good question. Could you tell me a little bit more about it?" By encouraging children to restate their questions, we are more likely to find out what they really want to know — and less likely to answer the questions in terms of what these questions mean to *us*.

Here is an example of what happens when a parent answers too quickly.

Seven-year-old Betsy came home from school and asked, "Mother, why do we go to our church and not St. Anne's?"

"Oh, dear," answered her mother in a horrified tone, "we would *never* go to the Catholic church. Catholics believe so many things that aren't true!"

Now, from the report of another conversation, it is clear that what Betsy really wanted to know was why she had to go to a different Sunday school from the one to which her two best friends went. Not only did this, her real question, remain unanswered, but she went away with a new question in her mind: "What awful things do Catholics believe that aren't true?"

Since children do not know what beliefs are denoted by the word "religious," Betsy did not know what one might believe in this area that wasn't true. Moreover, she did not even know of the existence of such beliefs as the immaculate conception or the infallibility of the Pope, which were perhaps what her mother had in mind.

A few days later Betsy announced soberly to a friend, "I wouldn't be a Catholic. They believe in Santa Claus." This, she had figured out, was something "not true" that one could be guilty of believing. And guilty she felt! For she realized that until very recently she had been just such a "Catholic" herself, and it was something Mother obviously did *not* approve of. Yet Mother had taught this belief to her. How confusing!

By allowing children time to tell us a little more about their questions, we may also catch a glimpse of the situations that occasion them. How did the question come up? Did a playmate say something, or an adult neighbor, a teacher, or someone on television? The weight carried by the words of each of these varies. If, without giving children a feeling that we are putting them off or subjecting them to the third degree, we can encourage them to talk a little more about what they are asking, it will increase the chance of our finding out what is really uppermost in their minds.

In a general discussion of children's questions, Gesell and Ilg warn:

"To begin with, he doesn't ask the questions all at once. He asks in relation to a specific spot on the frontier of *his* unknown. If you try to tell him too much and too early, you are more likely to bewilder him." [1] With religious questions, as with questions about sex, because we know how vast, complex, and controversial the subject is, we must be careful not to flood children with information and problems that are relevant and important for us but not for them. We should answer their questions in terms of the particular stage in their development, not expecting the answers to be adequate for a lifetime.

Another helpful approach is to clarify, both for ourselves and for the children, the *kind* of question under discussion. Is it a question largely of fact? Or is it, as is often the case with questions about religion, a mixture of fact and value? Or is it a question of almost pure speculation — what philosophers call a metaphysical question? These groups are like the colors of the rainbow: they merge into each other and yet are distinguishable.

"Did Jesus get killed?" This is a clear question of fact. How does one go about finding out whether a statement of fact is true? Where can we go to discover the facts about Jesus' life? Is something accurate and true just because it is written in a book? Can children believe everything that grownups tell them? What if the grownups disagree?

"Was Jesus magic?" This common child's translation of the idea of Jesus as a supernatural figure is not merely a question of fact but implies value. What we need to know first is the kind of man Jesus was. And when we find out the facts about him, how do we evaluate him? This is a second kind of question, then — one not so easily answered and one that the child will ultimately have to answer for himself when he is ready and able to undertake such a study.

"What happens after you die?" This is a third kind of question. What evidence is relevant when one attempts to answer this? Here we move into the realm of speculation.

We can study the speculations of others, we can make our own speculations, but can we actually know with any certainty?

How do we prove a fact is true? How do we prove a value judgment is sound? Is there any proof of metaphysical statements? These are things we will have to think about ourselves if we are going to help our children think about them. If we have never done it before, let's enjoy the fun of thinking about it with them.

It can bring satisfaction to children to be helped to see that there are these different kinds of questions, calling for different ways of being answered. It may save them from the hopelessly circular and highly emotional arguments that haunted the childhood of some of us.

One mother invented a game to alert her children to these distinctions.

"Is the African violet on the center of the table pretty? What kind of question is this?"

"Was Daddy home for supper last night? Were we ourselves before we were born? What kinds of questions are these?"

Sorting out such questions proved to be a stimulating pastime. Although the labels "fact," "value," and "metaphysics" were a little too stiff for the six-year-old, the nine-year-old enjoyed using them. The six-year-old explained, when it was his turn, whether he would answer a certain question by (a) looking it up in a book "or something"; (b) thinking of how it made him feel; (c) doing some more wondering.

If our children's questions are simple factual ones and call primarily for further information, we will want to direct the children to the proper sources if they are old enough to do some research. If we must give them the information ourselves, we should be careful not to give them more than they need. But let us be on guard here, for sometimes in our eagerness to stimulate children's questioning and steer clear of dogmatism, we are careless about knowing or finding out the purely factual aspects of a problem.

There is a difference between a fruitful questioning and a kind of wallowing in vague wondering that leads nowhere. An article describing "the new kind of Sunday School that encourages children to explore with their teacher the joyful mystery of being alive" reported the following conversation. It took place in a class of seven-year-olds.[2]

"What was there when there was nothin', just nothin'?" asked one boy.

"Well," said another boy, "when God came it was just there."

"What was there?" asked the first questioner.

"Just nothin', but when God came it turned into space. Maybe there was gas all around. Maybe the gas blew up and the earth was there after the blowup 'cause God wanted it that way. Then there was a lot more planets made by Him like He's always making them."

"Well," commented the first boy, "if He's always making them, then someday we can go from one to another with stepladders and that will be fun." He paused for a moment and added, "But I still want to know what was there when there was nothin'."

The article continued: "The teacher guided the discussion into the wonders of the Universe as evident in the moon, the stars, the planets. Rather wistfully she said, 'It's really a wonderful thing. It makes me wish I were an astronomer.'"

In our eagerness to let children think for themselves, there is a danger of being unnecessarily vague. Are planets "always being made"? Elsewhere, perhaps — but not in our solar system. Might it not have been a more productive experience for those boys and girls if the teacher had challenged the statement about how God is always making planets — if she had guided the group into a little research in simple astronomy? Then they could have made distinctions among what we *do* know, what we may someday know, and what it appears we can never know. To be an adequate liberal religious teacher or parent demands more information and more clear thinking than is demanded of those who unquestioningly hand on authoritarian beliefs.

Carelessness about searching for facts, when facts are called for, may result in a display of sloppy sophistication by our children. A father reports this remark of his eleven-year-old son who had been attending a liberal church school for three years: "I don't believe that Jesus ever lived, since he couldn't come back from the dead."

The father comments: "He seemed skeptical of religious teaching. I was deeply discouraged that we teach skepticism before simple elementary truths. At least our Sunday schools should teach the facts about our religion." Of course, because of the mixture of fact and myth that surround the person of Jesus, it is understandable how the son might feel he must reject the whole story. But we should be careful to teach our children to distinguish questions that are largely factual from those that call for something other than information.

Carelessness about knowing the facts may also be a contributing factor in a commonly reported urge among young liberals for a more specific and less vague religion. We should be very careful, too, when we use the device of answering children by asking them further questions. Unless we ask the right kind of question we may give children a feeling of being lost in a sea of ignorance.

Many of our children's religious questions involve a complicated mixture of fact and value. Is the Old Story of Salvation the greatest story ever told? We should try to show our children that the answer to that question requires: (a) the knowledge of what that story is, (b) a decision of some kind as to the "truth" of this story, (c) a knowledge of other great stories, especially great religious dramas of other cultures. Only when these three requirements have been met have we a sound basis on which to make the value judgment as to whether this is the greatest story ever told. One of the tragic aspects of most orthodoxies — political as well as religious — is the way in which they encourage children to assert blindly the unique value of their particular brand of truth without first training children in the hard task of developing standards of criticism.

"Daddy, do we hate McCarthy?" asked an eight-year-old hopefully. "Joey's family does. We do, don't we?"

"Do you know McCarthy?" asked his father. "Do you know anything about him?"

"No," said the little boy, hesitating, "but we do hate him, don't we? I told Joey I did."

What about the questions at the other end of the spectrum, so to speak — the questions that are largely metaphysical, the questions for which there seem to be no definite answers? How can we handle these without going beyond what we think can be said with certainty, and yet in such a way as to bring satisfaction?

"Mommy, do you think there is a Heaven?" asked six-year-old Freddy. "Tommy says there is."

Freddy's mother felt that the question of whether there is a heaven is not one that should be decided on the grounds of what one's mother, or one's church, says. So she answered like this:

"Freddy, let me ask *you* something. What happens when a person dies?"

"Well, his heart stops beating and his body stops working. Grandpa's did."

"What happens to his talking?"

"That stops, too," said the little boy.

"Can a person who has died tell us whether he has gone to Heaven?"

"No," said Freddy.

"Can anyone tell us what happens after we die?"

"Of course not."

"Then we just don't know," said his mother. "Some people like to think there is a lovely place called Heaven that we go to, but no one really knows."

By handling Freddy's question in this way his mother helped him to see the basis on which she felt an answer to this kind of question might be arrived at. Freddy saw that his mother was not less informed than Tommy, but that she felt this kind of question just can't have any more definite answer.

One afternoon four girls, between six and eight years old, sat around a table, drawing pictures. Two of them came from a Roman Catholic home, and the other two were from a family of religious liberals. The conversation took place at the home of the latter.

"God is only in our church," commented Mary. "Sister says so."

"Oh, no, God is in all churches," replied one of the children from the liberal home.

"No," said Maureen, "God is only in our church. Isn't God only in the Catholic church, Mrs. Peirce?"

"Well," said the mother, "I think God is in every church, but people have different ways of worshipping."

"I'll ask Sister tomorrow," said Mary. "I'm sure she said God was only in our church."

The mother reports: "At the time, I would have liked to convince these other children of what I believe. As I look back I realize that that was not my job, and the important thing for me to do was to show *my* children how I felt."

This was indeed one value, to have her own children realize how she felt. But would it not have been helpful to ask the children, all of them, how anyone can know where God is? If the Catholic children replied, "Because Sister tells us," the mother might have asked how the Sister knew where God is. Does God tell some people where He is, and not others? What do we mean when we use the word "God"?

Such a questioning approach might have helped the children to see that for a question such as this neither the authority of the Sister nor the authority of one's mother is the basis for an answer. Finding out about God is something, ultimately, that each must do for himself.

This brings up a concern expressed by many liberal religious parents — what they should do about religious questions asked by the neighbors' children. What should we say when these children bring their questions to us, or when we are present at a theological discussion among a group of children? If our opinion is requested or if we can comment on their discussion naturally and easily, should we do so? Or should we remain silent?

Some of these children may sense that from the liberal religious adult they will get a straightforward answer that might be denied them at home. Have we not just as much right as our orthodox friends to witness to the truth as we see it? If we are silent before the dogmas of orthodoxy, our own children will certainly feel that their friends have a special pathway to religious knowledge that, for some reason, is denied their family. A commonly reported remark among children is: "Well, Catholics know best."

Yes, we must take a positive stand. But we must at the same time respect the level of maturity of the children involved and show our belief in a method of inquiry and the democratic process as a means of arriving at truth.

In the incident just mentioned the mother might have had a more liberalizing influence if she had asked a mind-stretching question instead of giving an authoritative answer, even though it was a "liberal" answer. The children might then have had a brief glimpse of the exhilarating experience religious thinking can be, in contrast to their usual experience of asking someone higher up for the "right" answer.

It seems to us that, when the situation naturally presents itself, we have as much right to stretch the minds and sympathies of our children's friends as their parents have the right to confuse our children and necessitate the writing of this book.

One evening at bedtime, Donald, aged seven, asked his mother a question. He had been digging in the backyard with a Catholic friend, also seven.

"Billy says if you dig far enough you will find the Devil. Mama, is it true that there is a Devil? Billy's mother says there is."

Donald's mother felt that he sounded a bit frightened. She wanted to be reassuring.

"Donald, many people believe many different things. But scientists have dug deeply into the earth and found only rocks and dirt and water. Still the old superstitions about the Devil exist. You'll often hear the words 'Devil' and 'Hell.' 'Hell' is where the devil is supposed to live down under the earth."

"But, Mama," persisted Donald, "Billy says his mother told him there *is* a Devil. And if you do bad things the Devil gets you when you're dead! Who is right, his mother or you?"

"Tell me," said his mother, "what do *you* feel is the answer?"

"Gee, how should I know," said Donald helplessly. "Everybody says something different. But I guess there isn't really a Devil that you can dig down and find. Anyway I told Billy that there wasn't any."

The mother reported later that she did not think Donald was satisfied; if she had it to do over again, she would be more definite in her rejection of the idea of the Devil in order to reassure her child more fully.

It was probably a mistake for Donald's mother to ask, "What do *you* feel?" in reaction to his question. As the question was stated, Donald didn't know what kind of evidence would have been proof one way or the other. All he could *feel* at first hand was the weight of his mother's word against that of Billy's mother.

Also, unless used carefully, the phrase "What do you feel or think?" can suggest that the parent is as mystified as the child is; or that perhaps Billy's mother is right, although we don't think so. There are certain things that Donald's mother *can* know that Donald cannot: she can know why people have believed in the Devil. She can know the salvation story, in which the Devil plays a major role. She can know, too, that life has a dimension of evil in it with which Donald, as yet, hasn't had much experience, but that the idea of the Devil was intended to explain. To interpret orthodox beliefs adequately, she must begin to get some of this across to Donald.

Because of the way this mother answered, her child may not have felt that the question troubling him had really been answered. His friend Billy could always reply that Donald and the scientists hadn't dug deep enough! Actually, didn't this mother have cause and effect twisted around here? The existence of the Devil was not disproved because scientists dug in the earth; it was, rather, that the scientific world view just didn't include the Devil.

Belief in the literal existence of the Devil died out for most of the Western world when the scientific mentality took over. "The desire to construct a world-picture out of facts superseded the older ambition to weave a fabric of 'values' in which things and events were interpreted as manifestations of good and evil, related to powers, will, minds." [3]

In this instance would it not have been more reassuring to answer the child by relating the idea of the Devil to the earlier thought worlds in which it grew up? The Devil could then be understood not as a being whose existence must be proved or disproved, but as a character in an old story-way of understanding experience.

What were those early peoples trying to understand when they talked of devils and evil spirits? Sickness and natural catastrophes, hateful human actions, even death seemed to them to indicate that powerful, unfriendly gods were at war in the world with friendly gods and spirits. We have quite different ways now of understanding these events in our experience. Donald's mother might have explored a little with him some of the new ways of explaining sickness, earthquakes, jealousy. This kind of approach removes the necessity of pitting authority against authority; it enables the child to begin to find out for himself.

Actually, if we liberal religious parents but realize it, we are more fortunate than parents who accept traditional beliefs. Very probably an orthodox mother, when asked by her six-year-old son whether she believes in Heaven, feels a moral obligation to hand on the faith. For a while it will be enough for her child to accept the truth of the belief because Mother says it. But our scientifically oriented culture will threaten this belief as soon as her boy begins to sort out the real from the make-believe. Between six and eight he will probably relinquish his belief in Santa Claus, Superman, Heaven, and possibly God as taught at his mother's knee. Gesell and Ilg report of some seven-year-olds: "There are beginnings of slight skepticism about Santa Claus, about religion and other matters of which he has been told but which he has not experienced at first hand." [4]

In earlier times in a culture made up of one people, with one history, a single religious system gradually provided the framework in terms of which all life was interpreted and lived. Whether one was planting corn, going to war, caring for the sick, getting married, or dying, the over-arching religious system provided ways of thinking about these things. It prescribed acts to be done, songs to be sung, prayers to be said. When the old grandmothers explained what the moon was, what a comet was, where one went after death, all was explainable in terms of the religious myth. In such a world one could "hand on the faith" without having it threatened by a differently oriented system of thought. The growing child soon came to experience life in terms of the myth; so the myth was never contradicted by experience. There are few spots left in the world today where this is still true.

Today children in the civilized world must test their experience with minds fashioned by a different thought world than the one that shaped the faith of their fathers. It has been said that "the mind like all other organs can draw its sustenance only from the surrounding world."[5] For our minds the surrounding world is the thought world of the twentieth century. The thought world of the twelfth century and earlier is no longer nourishing. Because in our liberal religious church schools and homes we are encouraging our children to fashion a religious philosophy out of their own immediate experience, they need not go through the period of skepticism reported by Gesell and Ilg. Our children's religion is not something "of which he has been told but which he has not experienced at first hand." That is the glory of it.

Therefore, we can acquaint our children, during their pre-adolescent and adolescent years, with the myths, legends, cosmic dramas, stories of salvation, of all the world's cultures, presenting them as the ways other peoples had of understanding life. But we do not expect children of today to believe them.

When we do introduce these older ways of understanding experience, we want to be sure to introduce them from a variety of cultures, so that our children can have the data they need on which to base their thinking. Not just the myths, legends, and story of salvation from our Bible, but the myths, legends, and stories from all over the world must be the heritage of our children. They will be able to draw freely on any of these old ways for rich insights, and they may discard freely from any as they see fit.

We must constantly emphasize to our children that, although we may offer them our knowledge of facts and our help in sorting out kinds of questions and although we may seek to expose them to values that we hold high, the burden of discovery and the appropriation of truth rests ultimately on their own shoulders.

> You shall no longer take things at second or third hand, nor look through the eyes of the dead, nor feed on the spectres in books,
> You shall not look through my eyes either, nor take things from me,
> You shall listen to all sides and filter them from yourself.[6]

PART TWO

7

Traditional Teachings About God

"Who was God's father?"

Surely some of the most perplexing and persistent questions that our children put to us are questions about the word "God." They ask these questions not because they have been confronted with some reality that they cannot understand, but because they have heard this word used in confusing ways.

Whatever the reality that the word "God" expresses, God is not a simple concrete object of experience — nor something that one sees, hears, or touches, and about which one asks, "What is this?" For many religious liberals, concepts of God may be thought of as philosophic and poetic ways of summing up our thoughts and feelings about life.

When the idea of God is thought of in this way, it is important to ask: By what age are children likely to have had a rich enough experience and enough command of abstract thought and non-literal meaning to have their own understanding and appreciation of life enriched by the use of this word? Some of us who have been experimenting in new ways in religious education believe that to introduce the word "God" to help a child express his own understanding and appreciation of experience much before the age of ten is rarely successful. When introduced earlier than this, it may confuse more than enlighten, and stunt the child's own developing thoughts and feelings.

We believe, however, that the *experiences* out of which

conceptions of God grow are available to children from the moment of birth. In our positive program of religious education with young children, therefore, we seek to accent the religious values latent in all experience without using the word God.

Even when children reach an age at which they can naturally use the word "God" in relation to their own feelings and thoughts about life, we cannot give them a concept of God for their own. We can acquaint them with other peoples' ideas of God, including our own, but we cannot bequeath to them our idea or anyone else's. That must, by our definition, be the fruit of their own living.

Of course, we must face the fact that our children hear the word "God" used in a variety of ways long before the age of ten. Our concern, then, must be to help them find, if possible, meaningful content for the concepts they hear, even though we believe that they are not ready to use the word in relation to their own deep insights and feelings.

We must admit that the definition of the idea of God that we have suggested is very different from the most commonly accepted idea of God. Also our suggestion that children ideally should not be expected to use this word about their own experience until they are capable of mature thought and feeling is very different from what has been the traditional approach to the subject.

The idea of God or the gods that was taught to even the youngest children in most cultures in the past was not abstract or non-literal. With all the vividness they could muster, the elders in a culture taught the new generation about the powers that ruled the universe. Everything that happened was explained as the action of God, or the gods, or evil spirits. Children needed to know about these powers in order to understand sun and moon, flood and famine, birth and sickness and death. Children needed to know about them in order to behave in ways pleasing to the gods. Fear of the gods was encouraged and used as a method of controlling children's behavior. Belief in the gods gave strength to those who had to live in a precarious world.

Contemporary primitive cultures and the stricter orthodoxies of our day still attempt to teach the idea of God in this way. But the majority of modern parents, if they were to speak frankly, would admit to finding the idea of God increasingly difficult to teach convincingly to the young.

This is because, as mentioned before, our whole modern way of thinking and feeling is permeated with another way of looking upon and interpreting the facts of our experience. Instead of beginning with the premise that everything that happens is the result of the will of supernatural powers, we begin by assuming that events are the result of an interplay of various natural forces, economic, social, political, psychological, physical. These forces are increasingly predictable and susceptible to control.

We live in a world, therefore, that has come to rely on life insurance, not Providence; on penicillin, not prayer. Today we know that germs, not evil spirits, cause sickness; that pressure areas, not supplications, bring rain. We know that fear and worry cause emotional problems and that by talking about them we may help to cast them out. We know that, if the end comes, it is more likely to be through man-made hydrogen bombs than by God-made fire and brimstone. In a thought world of such explanations it is increasingly difficult to feel a real dependence on a supernatural God who enters the universe from outside or above us.

Then what shall be done about the idea of a supernatural God ruling and overruling the universe, as an explanation for things as they are or as a way of reconciling one's feelings to whatever comes for evil or good?

Contemporary religious orthodoxy, especially the Protestantism of educated men and women, is uncertain. The sophisticated teachers of religious thought in Protestantism conceive of God in terms that would have very little reality to laymen, and perhaps would be quite shocking to them. Paul Tillich, who is at present considered one of the profoundest Protestant thinkers by clergy and intellectual laymen, writes: "God, in contrast to everything else, is not given. He is not something which we can find in the context of reality. He does not appear as an object beside other objects. He is not a being beside other beings, within the totality of our world." [1]

Such theologians cannot literally believe in an anthropormorphic God (a God who is like a human being), but they are content to use all the old words about God, explaining them as merely symbolic. This makes it possible for such men to remain within the orthodox churches. At the same time, most lay people are left to use the old words, or none, unaware of the intellectual reinterpretations of such men as Dr. Tillich. This means that most laymen see but two alternatives. Either they use the old words with the old meanings, gaining what emotional support they can from them and separating off into different compartments their religious thinking and their everyday intellect; or they give up the old words, and, because they think that without these words there can be no religion, they live without the emotional support that a vital religion ought to give.

In either case the majority of such persons feel at an even greater loss when it comes to solving the problem of how to answer their children's first searching questions. Whether to deal with them scientifically or religiously they do not know. This is one reason for the increasing enrollment in the church schools. Parents who are a little frightened in our insecure world yearn for the support of religion; they want their children to gain more support from it than they do. With this hope they send their children to learn about God at church school where the "experts," who know about such things, can teach their children. The parents hope that what the children learn will be convincing and coherent with the rest of life.

In an increasing number of church schools, teachers use curricula that have been worked out by denominational leaders who are aware of the reinterpretations of the leading theologians, but who also are aware, to a degree, of the mental and emotional capacities and needs of children at various ages. The result is that in a good many church schools what children are taught about God is very confusing. They are not urged to believe in the vivid old God ruling with love and wrath over a predominantly evil world — nor are they taught anything radically different.

What is the idea of God that gets through to the majority of children trained in traditional Sunday schools? It is mostly a watered-down version of the old theology. In spite of learned theological controversies among top theological thinkers of various faiths, the traditional idea of God that sifts through to children tends to be simple, uniform, and self-contradictory.

God is a person, a man, without a body. He cannot be seen or touched, and yet He can be talked to. This is called praying. You can ask Him for things, and yet you aren't supposed to exactly. If you are good, you may get what you ask for, and then again you may not. He knows what is best for you. He lives in Heaven. That is where dead people are with God. Jesus is there, too, only he isn't dead. God is also everywhere, but especially in churches, and at the same time He is in everyone. He was also Jesus. God wants people, especially children, to be good, and He punishes bad people, and yet He forgives them. He can see and hear everything and keeps track of everything you do. He plans for everything. God made everything and makes the rain come now and makes things grow. We aren't to blame Him for hurri-

canes and accidents and prayers that don't get answered —
we just don't know all about God yet. God likes to have
people thank Him a lot.

Most children of four and five are intrigued with these
ideas when they first hear them. They ask very detailed and
very inappropriate questions about them. "How long a
ladder do you need to get up to God?" "Does God have
levers He pulls to make it rain and snow?" "Why did God
make it rain for our picnic?" "Why did God kill my new
puppy with that car?" "Who was God's father?"

Volumes could be composed of these questions, showing
the tragic confusion produced in young minds as the inevitable result of these attempts to teach little children about
God. It is tragic for two reasons. First of all, the teachings
cause the children to waste their wonderful gift of curiosity
on asking questions that are not about their own first-hand,
unadulterated experience, but about this mysterious word.
The word has been given as an explanation; but, instead of
explaining anything, it produces problems that are without
any solution, because the children necessarily misunderstand
what the adult has meant by this God and His attributes.
The result of this is that, instead of religion being an exhilarating exploration of their expanding worlds, for many children religion is all mixed up with unanswerable and often
emotionally upsetting conundrums. "Well, if God made the
world, who made God?" "If God can see everything I do
and if He can do anything, why does He let me be so bad?"
Instead of being spiritually nourished by the realities available to any age, children are being spiritually sickened by
ideas they cannot make their own.

It is tragic, secondly, because children have been given
these teachings by their parents or teachers out of predominantly good motives. The motives are to help children better
understand life, to face its trials and tribulations more
bravely, to be better-behaved boys and girls. The time has

come for someone to study systematically the effect of such teachings on children. Are children so taught better able to understand their world? Are they better able to cope with adversity? Are they better-behaved boys and girls than those who have not been so indoctrinated?

After a study of several reports [2] of the religious attitudes and concepts of children between the ages of four and eight, exposed to traditional religious teachings about God, we suggest that there are several counts on which traditional teachings, as they are understood by children, must be seriously questioned.

(1) The ideas, although meant to help children better understand life, actually spread intellectual confusion. Much that children learn as religious truths they will have to unlearn at a later date. "Mrs. Smith said that Jesus is up in Heaven with God," says Harry. "But the sun is up there and would burn them both up." Clever theologians may neatly solve the battle between science and religion on a verbal level, but their neat solutions are lost on children.

(2) Although taught in order to help children better appreciate God's wonderful world and orderly universe, these ideas actually impede the slow development of children's awareness of natural laws. If they consider God capable of magic, they cannot respect or appreciate the actual order and law in nature. "I guess if God makes babies, He runs out of them sometimes, 'cause Aunty Jean doesn't have one." "God can make me well in time for my party, even if the doctor says I have to stay in bed another day." "Why doesn't God put out that forest fire?" "God ought to move that mountain nearer our house."

(3) Although taught to help children to be good, these traditional beliefs may actually lessen a child's sense of being responsible for his own actions. "If God sees me, why does He let me act bad?" "When the Devil wants it, he makes me bad." "I'll ask God to make me gooder after tomorrow."

(4) Although children are given traditional teachings in order to help them feel secure in the universe, many orthodox teachings are emotionally frightening, especially to a child who is already upset. "Little children are afraid of God. . . . They get the wrong impression. God made the flood. It might come again." "I don't want God to see me all the time." "You know, I used to think that if you didn't say your prayers, God did something to you, but He doesn't. I tried it."

(5) These teachings give children the idea that their natural needs and developing capacities are at war with God. "God doesn't want me to fight with my brother, but I want to." "We mustn't run through God's house."

(6) These teachings make God actually hateful to many children. "I don't like God. He was mean to make His Son die." "If I go to God's house, why doesn't He come out and let me see Him?" "I hate God for making that hurricane." "God took my Daddy, but I want my Daddy here."

(7) Ideas of God as traditionally taught often produce in children a dogmatic sureness, which they will either desperately cling to the rest of their lives or utterly reject when revolt sets in. These lines from a poem were read to a group of children: "No one can tell me, nobody knows, where the wind comes from, where the wind goes." One child remarked indignantly, "Why, it comes from God, of course." Is not the poet with his wistful query closer to an experience of God than the child with his glib answer?

The idea of God is too important, the reality of God too available, children themselves too wonderful, for this confusion to be either right or necessary. Somewhere a mistake is being made.

Often we are told that, because children of four and five think concretely and cannot think abstractly, they must be given a very specific idea of God, even though they may have to outgrow it. If the idea of God, as we adults are able to use it, is abstract or poetic or non-literal, then are we not saying that it is an idea that young children by definition cannot handle without distorting and misunderstanding it?

Surely we would agree that children think concretely. But is not the implication of this that therefore we must let them have specific and tangible experiences and the concepts that are appropriate to these and wait until they can handle the concept of God? We do not hurry impatiently to hand on the philosophic concepts of a God-intoxicated Spinoza or the poetic insights of a God-filled Whitman to feed our children's spirits. Why must we hurry so with the finest thoughts of God of the Psalmists or of the prophets or of Jesus?

Children would be far more richly rewarded if parents and teachers made less effort to give them the word "God," and more effort to share with them experiences contributing to curiosity and wonder. We do not believe that children should have to discard early, immature concepts of God; rather, through spiritually nourishing experiences, they should develop an ever-deepening concept.

8

Interpreting Ideas of God

"Is God real, like kings, or make-believe, like giants?"

The children of religious liberals may be spared direct in-
doctrination in the confusion described in the preceding
chapter, and yet they may be just about as confused as their
friends as a result of the impact of the culture upon them.

A young father listened to this conversation between his
four-year-old daughter Nancy and her friend Amy. Nancy
had been told nothing about God.

"You know, if you kill someone, God will punish you," said
Amy.

"Who is God?" asked Nancy.

"Oh," said Amy, who was very clear on this point, "God
is dead and He's inside of you."

The teaching that God is somehow in each of us, and that
Jesus was divine, had come to a sad end here! Actually it is
this kind of confused theology that serves as an introduction
to the idea of God for many of our children. What can we
and should we do about this?

There are three things in particular that might be done.
First of all, we can introduce at an early age the idea that
"God" is a word that is not easily understood. Different
people use the word differently to express their understanding and feelings about the world. Some people prefer not to
use the word at all.

Second, we can try to relate the word, once our children
hear it and are concerned about it, to vital experiences that
they themselves have been having.

And, third, if the word is being used in a way that is utterly foreign to our use of it or is outside the children's own experience, we can attempt to re-create the thought world of those who use it in this way, and thus interpret to our children the meaning it has or had for those so using it.

Let us begin with the first suggestion — to emphasize that "God" is a word that is not easily understood. It seems unfortunate for a child to start out with the idea that God is some*one* whose existence must be either affirmed or denied, especially some*one* with such confusing attributes.

Writes one mother: "My child gets more and more cynical about the possibility of a God as the stories she hears from her orthodox friends and her teacher at school become more impossible for her to digest. She loves the curriculum in our liberal church school, and I hate to have religion spoiled for her by the fantastic things she hears from these friends." It is ironic that the impatience of the orthodox to propagate their faith often turns our children against ideas like God and prayer.

How necessary it is, then, that we try to establish with children the attitude, right from the beginning, that "God" is a word that different people use differently. People in various parts of the world, over the centuries, have also used it very differently. One interesting thing our children can study in the years ahead is the variety of ways in which the word "God" has been used.

If this approach is taken, children will not spend years trying to feel something called God that exists somehow "out there." This something, unlike everything else that exists, can neither be seen, nor felt, nor heard, nor touched, nor tasted, nor smelled. Most children, if they could speak up frankly, would admit to feeling a little guilty that they don't exactly feel this very important Being who is so much talked about.

One second-grade teacher asked if any of the children could tell how one "might know the nearness of God."

A seven-year-old girl said, "Well, you relax sort of, get real quiet, listen, real quiet — and then when you're all relaxed you sort of feel Him near."

A boy spoke up. "Yeah, but what if you fall asleep?"

The girl immediately answered, "Then you dream about Him, silly." [1]

This is not, to our way of thinking, the kind of attitude we wish to encourage. One of the plagues of religion throughout the ages has been its unreality and its encouragement of hypocrisy and pretense. Religion is supposed to be concerned with what is most real, most honest, most poignant. The reality that we understand by the concept "God" is a part of children's experience when they have their eyes wide open and their minds alert.

Let us remove from children the uneasy fear that they are not feeling or thinking what they are supposed to think or feel when they hear the word "God." Let us impress upon them, instead, the adventure that lies ahead as they try to discover what men in different times and places have meant by the word "God." They will accept or reject what they honestly must in the various interpretations.

Because we want to establish this attitude, we should possibly look for occasions with children, even as young as four, to suggest that "God" is this kind of a word. We do this, not with the expectation that they will use it of their own experience, but in order that their first introduction to the word will be positive and not some confused anthropormorphism handed on by a friend.

In the story "Still Finding Out," in *The Family Finds Out*,[2] a book for five-year-olds, Ellen asks what the word "God" means. She has heard it used in a song. Her mother suggests that God means different things to different people, but that the word has to do with our wondering about life.

Her mother says it may mix Ellen up for awhile, but that she has her whole life to try to understand about God. The result is that Ellen is helped to feel more secure even though she lacks a concrete meaning for the word.

Our second suggestion is that we should try to relate the word "God," when the child seems concerned about it, to experiences that the child himself has had that might throw light on some of the meanings contained in the word.

One mother had suggested to her four-year-old son David that the word "God" might be thought to mean the same thing as the word "life" or the word "nature." One day David came in from playing with a small friend. They had apparently been talking about God.

David burst out, "God is life, isn't He?" And then, before his mother could gather her resources to make an answer, he went on, "Is God real like kings or make-believe like giants?"

"God is very real, David," said his mother. "But at our house we don't think of God as a man, but more like nature and what makes all things grow." (The mother later commented: "I knew the word 'nature' had meaning for him because we use it over and over as we watch the growth of our chicks, and new baby, and plants.")

To David she went on and said, "If we say God is life, or God is nature, we surely think God or nature is real, for we see the growth of things and know something very real is taking place."

Then, because the mother felt she was sounding a little wordy, she and David went out together to a maple tree near the house. They had been watching it daily, even hourly, as the buds unfolded. David was excited to see how much more the leaves had opened. While he held the branch his mother said: "Perhaps we could say that this is God."

The mother later reported: "David had made almost no comment while I talked. He watched my face with interest and I think perhaps was somewhat puzzled. I don't know that he was satisfied, and I don't know that I cleared up the misconception as to whether God was real or not. It will take a great many questions and probably several years to begin to clarify this in David's mind, but I feel sure he will ask again and again."

Because this mother had been giving her boy vital religious experiences, she was able to turn to these experiences and attempt to relate the word "God" to them. However, children think concretely, and it may well be that David thought God *was* the maple branch. The mother was trying to point to a process, but a child does not naturally verbalize a process.

We do not suggest *introducing* the concept of God, even when relating it to the child's experience, as a positive policy in the liberal church or home, for children as young as four or five. But when the child comes in with a question, as David did, or if for some other reason the child seems to need this further content, then one might do something similar to what this mother did. But because of the almost inevitable over-simplification and misunderstanding that occurs, we prefer to give children *experiences* of God early and hold off using the word about their experiences as long as possible.

The three "Martin and Judy" books, written for three- to five-year-olds, present the vital day-by-day experiences of two children, with the relevant religious values highlighted. The concept of God is not introduced until the third book. In an attempt to build up a meaning for this concept, the idea of a "wonder-part" was introduced in the second "Martin and Judy" volume. The wonder-part, it was suggested, was the invisible aliveness that is in us and that somehow leaves the body after we die. It is in birds, and spiders, and all living things. In the third volume this suggestion is made: "Perhaps all the many wonder-parts in things everywhere, and in everybody, are really just One Great Wonder-Part. Sometimes we call this One Great Wonder-Part by another name. We say God." [3]

Many parents and teachers using these stories have come to feel that, in spite of every precaution, children misunderstand this concept, just as they misunderstand the adult concept of God. Children, thinking in the only way they can, ask, "Where is my wonder-part? In my stomach, my head, or where?" Many parents and teachers, therefore, prefer to omit this concept that may be misunderstood and to concentrate on the *experiences* that children do not misunderstand.

The "Martin and Judy" stories stress another idea that does seem to us to lay a helpful groundwork for children's spiritual growth and ultimately for an understanding of the idea of God. This is the emphasis on the thought that for something to be *real* it does not have to be seen or touched. Judy plays a game with her father in which she tries to touch — that is, test for its reality — Daddy's love. [4] She touches his eyes, ears, nose, and so on; but she cannot touch his love. Even a four-year-old can see the point — that the word *real* can be used to describe something intangible: the beauty of a flower, the love of a parent.

On an older age level, this same idea is developed in the story "The Questions of King Malinda" in the volume *From Long Ago and Many Lands*. [5] Perhaps it can be suggested to a child that for some people the word "God" has meant the vital force that lies behind the living Universe. This vital force is real, and yet it cannot be seen or touched, though the created Universe itself can.

In *The Child From Five to Ten*, Gesell and Ilg and their associates have a final section on the child's developing philosophic outlook and religious concepts. [6] They suggest that the person of Santa Claus "may prove to be a bridge to the concept of God as a creator and governor." We would strenuously disagree with this suggestion. There are few homes in which Santa Claus is introduced as a pretend or make-believe person right from the beginning. The child is usually told that Santa Claus is a real man who really visits our homes; only gradually, in some cases not until six or seven, do children see through the hoax and discover the truth. Because in most homes children have also been taught about God, whom they interpret to be magic in the same way as Santa Claus and Superman, these three magic figures are pictured as equals; they lose their credibility at about the same time, when the child is somewhere between six and ten. This is precisely the kind of shattering experience we do not wish for our children in relation to the idea of God.

Even in homes where Santa Claus is introduced as a mythical personification of the spirit of giving and good cheer, the myth makes a poor vehicle for the idea of God. It is precisely the anthropomorphic idea of God, as an old man with a long white beard, that we do not wish to have stunting and distorting our children's concept of God all through their lives.

It is in connection with real experiences with nature that children seem to be most helped to first catch a glimpse of the reality that is referred to by the word "God." We have not found that the analogy between God and a father was helpful with small children, since it seems to introduce more problems than it solves; but others may have had a different experience with this.

The story "Wondering About God," in *The Tuckers*, describes the kind of experience in relation to which a discussion of the idea of God is sometimes fruitful.[7] It is suggested that God may be thought of as what knows how to grow. The suggestion is also made that people have had very different ideas about God, and that this is something to challenge our curiosity and interest.

The collection *From Long Ago and Many Lands* contains

two other stories that have proved helpful at times. They may throw light on an abstract conception of God by relating the conceptions to something the children know in their own experience. The two stories, "The Fig Seed" and "The Lump of Salt," are from Indian sacred writings. In the former, the life that is in a seed, and yet cannot be seen when the seed is cut open, is compared to God in the Universe. The second story presents the idea that, just as a lump of salt, when dissolved in water, cannot be seen but can be tasted, so God, in the Universe, cannot be seen but is present in all things.

If children have heard and been puzzled by the idea that God is everywhere, these stories may help to reduce the confusion and fear that this idea sometimes causes. We suggest, however, that these two stories are quite subtle and should be reserved, if possible, until the age of nine or ten.

Another idea that children often find perplexing and possibly upsetting is the idea that God is all-powerful and can do anything. One mother, concerned to put some positive content in this notion, tried to accomplish this in the context of a real experience. She did this not primarily to teach the concept of God at the age of five, but in order to straighten out something that had confused her son.

Jerry had listened to a story[8] read to an older child, in which God was described as "the strongest thing in the world." The mother knew that the little boy was baffled by this. What was this God that was so strong? He had not felt it. He found the idea a little frightening.

A few days later Jerry and his mother were walking in the woods. The little boy was exclaiming about how much things had developed since their last walk. It was early spring. The buds were just bursting open on the bushes. The whole woods wore a yellow-green color.

"Nothing can stop spring now," said his mother. "It's really coming."

"Even if we *wanted* it to be winter again, we couldn't

make it be," said Jerry, excited at the idea of trying to *stop* spring.

"Just think of the millions of hands there would have to be to close up the buds and push the green sprouts back into the earth to make it winter again," suggested his mother.

"Why, it would take a thousand, thousand hands for just *this* woods," said the little boy. "And really you couldn't — it would push right through your fingers!"

"Maybe that's what the story was all about that we read the other night," said his mother. "You remember it said that God was the strongest thing in the world. Maybe the man who wrote that story was using the word God to mean what pushes the world awake in the spring." Thus Jerry's mother was helping him to find a way to think when he heard the word God.

But a word of caution should be said about using experiences with nature to give content to the word "God." Care should be taken that children are not given a one-sided view of nature or a man-centered (anthropocentric) view of nature. Whether nature is aware of, or has a special concern for, man — this is a question they will ask and answer for themselves over the years.

The fact that man's interests seem to be only part of nature's story was made vivid to one mother. She was floundering through a conversation with her five-year-old son on the subject of "religion."

"There certainly are a lot of things that we don't understand, aren't there?" she remarked. "Things that we wonder about."

"Yes," said Bruce, quietly and thoughtfully.

"Maybe we could speak of 'the wonder-part' instead of God when we try to think about what makes flowers and people and animals grow and live," continued his mother.

"I don't like black widow spiders and tarantulas," said Bruce vigorously.

"No," said his mother, "we don't like to have them where we are, do we?"

"I don't like God to make them. I don't like red ants either." (He had been bitten by them that afternoon.)

Nature is not all sweetness and light, and we should not start our children off with an attitude toward it that will cause them to recoil in horror when they take a second look.

A nine-year-old girl and her mother were walking in a field early in the morning. The dew showed up a beautiful web and a very large golden garden spider busily winding up a grasshopper that had been careless enough to get caught. The child and her mother watched as the spider went busily about its business of packaging its prey.

With a big sigh the nine-year-old finally said, "Well, I suppose the grasshopper had eaten someone else, and maybe a catbird will eat the spider!"

Whatever theology this little girl finally evolves, it will include *all* the facts about nature — not just the rosy-hued ones. An idea of God or a philosophy of life that ignores conflicts of interest in nature and human affairs — and the resulting suffering and fear and anger — is inadequate for any age level.

Are not many of the most perplexing questions that young children ask about God the result of giving children the idea that God has arranged the whole universe with man in mind? Is there really good evidence that we are the end product of a Great Plan?

The teaching that nature reveals God's plan, and that God plans for boys and girls to live in happy homes, and so forth, is a favorite emphasis in orthodox Sunday-school materials at present. But in many instances the plans do not seem to work out well. Alert children who learn of broken homes, displaced persons, hurricanes, tornadoes, and hydrogen bombs soon come to question this very neat theology. Of course, the doctrine of sin is called in to explain some of these discrepancies, as well as the idea that men have as yet only discovered part of this Great Plan.

After many years of first-hand observation, a child may well emerge as a youth convinced of a Plan behind creation; a Plan that had man as its goal and continues to have him as its special concern. Not everyone will agree with him, but he has a right to his personal theology. But to teach four- and five-year-old children dogmatically that nature reveals God's Plan seems to us to impose on children something that it is their privilege to search out for themselves.

A child, encouraged to watch the ant under his feet, the spider on the bush, will early find out a great deal about the Universe. In the "Martin and Judy" books the children do just this. They see the fly caught in the spider's web; to free the fly means to deprive the spider of his supper.[9] In such an experience children see first hand that conflicts of interest are basic to life, and that man, too, has his moments of being caught in the web of things. This approach, we feel, will help children to accept life in our Universe on a mature basis. They will not feel a need to rationalize everything that is not pleasing to man in general, and to themselves in particular.

In a study of the kind of pictures that junior-age children in an orthodox church school thought appropriate for a worship center, it was reported: "A universal choice for exclusion from a worship center was a color picture of a golden spider in the center of an intricate web. Spiders made most of the children express fear or revulsion. Some said, 'He looks peculiar. I know God created spiders and flies for some good reason, but I don't know why. The spider might be one who helps God by punishing those who do wrong.'"[10] If these children had not had their vision distorted by an anthropocentric theology, how differently they would have looked at these pictures! "And a mouse is miracle enough to stagger sextillions of infidels."[11]

Finally, as suggested at the beginning of this chapter, there will be times when children hear ideas of God that are both foreign to our understanding of the concept and removed from their own experience. We may wonder, for example, how to bridge the gap between the idea of God as a rather vague concept, and the talk of personified gods that is prevalent in myths. We may wonder how to make understandable to our children the notion of God as a very tangible being, without destroying their own gradually developing concept.

Perhaps a solution lies in going back with children, starting at about the age of six, to the very beginning of man's adventure on earth, back to the cave people. We may try to make vivid and real the kind of world in which the most primitive people probably lived. Without frightening our children, who hardly ever experience nature in the raw, we may re-create for them, in story form, a world in which storms, periods of hunger, death by violence were a real and continual threat.

Early man was afraid. He had to work out ways of keeping alive in a dangerous world. He watched and admired and possibly learned from the wild animals that roamed the earth and managed to survive. And because man is man, he not only thought and solved his practical problems, but evolved ways of expressing his feelings and thoughts about his world. This was his religion. It was also his science and his art. We may try to show children how early man interpreted the objects around him as Beings with wills and powers. The rocks, the trees, wind, sun, moon, sea — these were probably man's first gods. This we find we can explain to children without being misunderstood.

A book that will help us do this has not, to our knowledge, yet been written. It might be called *Beginnings of Faith and Worship*. Probably it should contain simple stories, based on the best evidence available, of what we imagine lay behind the earliest development of primitive god ideas in various parts of the world. Many students of child development believe that there are striking similarities between the way primitive men thought and the way children think. If this is so, it ought not to be too difficult for children to think themselves into this world, even though by the age of six they are already beginning to see experience through concepts shaped in a scientific area.

Many parents report that there seems to be a genuine curiosity in a child of five or six about "first things." Who took care of the very first baby? Where did the first seed come from? It is partly because children naturally ask these questions that many parents answer, "God," without giving the matter much thought. Having given so specific an answer, the parents are then overwhelmed by a series of very specific unanswerable questions.

A six-year-old asked his mother, "Where did the first dinosaur come from? Oh, I know he came from an egg, but where did the egg come from?"

"Well," said his mother, struggling to put her thoughts clearly, "there are some things that we simply don't know. The scientists have a way of explaining how one kind of life might turn into another kind, but it is too complicated to explain to you yet. But they believe that the first dinosaur might have come from a different kind of animal that just started laying eggs that gradually got to be more like dinosaurs."

"That's all right, Mommy," said the little boy. "I know we don't know the answers to questions like this, like where the first seaweed or the first fish came from. Don't worry, Mum, maybe I can help find out when I grow up!"

How much more stimulating for a child to be answered in some such way as this and to be encouraged in his curiosity than to be given, at the beginning of his own adventure in thought, the final and thought-stifling answer, "God made them." It is a fine thing for children to have their own wondering encouraged and appreciated. It will also deepen children's insight and widen their sympathies, if they are introduced to a few of the explanations that primitive men worked out to answer the same questions. In two books called *Beginnings of Earth and Sky* and *Beginnings of Life and Death,* written for nine- to eleven-year-olds, these early ways of understanding have been collected from ancient peoples all over the world.[12] Preceding each myth, there is a brief section giving historic material about the group from which the myth comes. The collection contains the old Bible myths of creation and the fall of man. Children with whom these stories are shared feel themselves standing in a line of wonderers extending far back in time and around the world.

Although these books have been prepared for children older than the six- and seven-year-olds whom we have in mind here, one or two of the myths from each book may be used to introduce children to this old way of thinking. The collection also contains a modern scientist's way of explaining the beginnings of things, and this we have found does have to wait to be used until children's thought has matured further.

Probably by the age of five or six our children will have heard their playmates talk of the first man and first woman that God made — Adam and Eve — and of how God made the whole world in six days. This is the appropriate time to suggest that the Adam and Eve story is just one such creation story, and that all peoples have had their stories of creation, their own wonderings about beginnings. If we put the Adam and Eve story in this comparative context, right from the beginning, children will not worry about whether it is true or false; they will see that it is an old way of thinking, giving one answer that one early people worked out. They may compare the Adam and Eve story with another in the collection, "The First Animals Make Men." This myth of the Mi-wok Indians is especially appealing to children and delights even six-year-olds.

Children with whom this approach is used, we find, do not have the idea that the old ways of thinking were inferior and that today we know the right answers to these hard questions. If we make the world of early men real and vivid, old ways of thinking are appreciated for the accomplishments they were. These early thinkers were keen observers, and children enjoy discovering how similar some of the early thoughts are to those of the most up-to-date scientists. They can appreciate the fact that the earliest thinkers had only their own experience to go by, and that we have inherited the best insights of men down through the ages.

Many of the traditional ideas that children bring from their friends can be handled by relating them to this old way of understanding. A six-year-old reported that his friend Henry had said, "God writes down all the bad things you do in a book." It is not enough to reply, "Oh, I don't believe that." We may go a little further and say something like this: "Some people think of God as being somewhat like a person who watches the world and keeps track of everything that is done. It's more like the way people used to think of the gods in the old myths and stories. I think one thing they are trying to say is that it really matters the kind of person that we are and that it is important to try to be fine people. I believe that; do you?"

Another approach we find helpful in trying to make personifications of God thinkable to six- and seven-year-olds is through culture heroes. In most early cultures, stories were told and retold of culture heroes, semi-divine beings who were probably a symbol of all men in their struggle against the elemental forces of nature. Some students of religion believe that these half-gods were forerunners of the more abstract concept of purely supernatural beings. Perhaps we need a collection of simplified tales of these culture heroes, such as Hiawatha and Maui and Gilgamesh.

The creation of culture heroes is not something that happened only in the dim dark past. It happened not so long ago in our own American culture, when men were again thrust into close contact with nature's forces. Paul Bunyan, hero of the lumberman; Pecos Bill, hero of the cowboys; Old Stormalong, hero of the whaling men — here is the same myth-making instinct functioning on our own American scene. These heroes were symbols of the pioneers themselves struggling against the elements. These heroes could really do what the pioneers wished they themselves could do. Although not of the cosmic dimensions of earlier culture heroes, they were more than men; they were supermen. *The Real Book of American Tall Tales* brings stories of these and other mighty men together under one cover in a style that six- to eight-year-olds can grasp and enjoy.[13]

Moreover, this myth-making instinct not only exhibits itself in the creation of mythical heroes, but also is at work when we create legends about real, historic heroes. From the patriarch Abraham to the almost contemporary Abraham Lincoln, history testifies to this poetic urge in man to say, through legends: "Here was a great man — no, more than a great man, a chosen one of God."

Children hearing the stories of culture heroes and legends about real human beings, can begin to have a way to think about miracles. Miracles are a symbol of the human longing to be free of our binding human limitations. Young children from five to seven do not think of miracles as a break in natural law, because they have no grasp of natural law as a system to be broken into. But they can feel the desirability of being able to walk a mile in a step, or to throw a lasso to the top of Pike's Peak, or to "kill a 'bar' when he was only three." Thinking about miracles in this way removes the worry of whether or not they really happened. When children do develop an awareness of natural law, there will be no clash between this and their esthetic enjoyment of myth.

If a few primitive myths, stories of culture heroes, and tall tales of folk heroes are introduced carefully, children of six and seven may be better able to understand what their orthodox playmates are talking about and taught to believe literally. But it is important that such material be used very carefully — and not used at all if it seems to mix children up. As stated earlier, children between three and eight need help in distinguishing between what can *really* happen, what we *wish* could happen, or what we *pretend* could happen. Our culture seems to go out of its way to confuse and frighten children — with Santa Claus, Superman, Pinocchio, Hansel and Gretel, giants, witches, men from Mars, all tossed in a jumble at them.

We believe that children should be encouraged to appreciate and enjoy the real, and to take pride in their real accomplishments. In our effort to make contemporary anthropomorphic ideas of God understandable, therefore, let us not cause further confusion. However, we find that, if handled carefully, the approach suggested can be helpful.

Five-year-old Mike, who had heard a good deal of this talked about with his seven-year-old sister Jane, opened a discussion with his mother.

"I am going to be a scientist when I grow up."

"Oh," said his mother, "that's interesting. That will make two in the family, because that's what Jane says she is going to be, too."

"A girl scientist!" said the little boy with scorn. "Who ever heard of a girl scientist?"

"Oh, yes," said his mother, "there have been lots of famous women scientists. There was a very famous one named Madame Curie."

"Is she dead?" asked Mike.

"Yes," said the mother, "she died some time ago."

"Have any legends grown up about her yet?" asked the little boy.

This mother felt that Mike was getting the point very nicely.

It is indeed difficult for almost any one of us to state clearly what the idea of God means to us. Is it surprising that it is infinitely more difficult to explain to children either what we mean, or what others of our contemporaries mean, or what men of the past have meant?

Our motive in attempting to interpret the idea of God to children is not to control their behavior and make them "good." Our hope is that children may come to appreciate the insights of men down through history, and to feel that the concept of God is one they may someday use to express their own insight into the meaning of life.

9

New Ways in Prayer

"One thing I am going to pray for is a night without any bad dreams."

A second group of perplexing questions and situations center around the traditional practice of prayer. Questions about prayer, of course, relate very closely to questions about God, and the way we deal with ideas of God will basically affect the way we deal with prayer.

If we believe that a concept of God necessarily develops very slowly over the years and that an early personification of the idea of God results in confusion and distortion in children's minds, then it will hardly seem logical to teach small children to say their prayers to God. Many liberal religious parents therefore do not start their children out in the traditional manner at two and three with a prayer to be said to God at night or at mealtime.

It is not only religious liberals, however, who are questioning the old patterns of prayer, but a large proportion of modern men and women. Prayer is something for which many people can more easily say a good word than practice sincerely. As was true of the idea of God, it is because new patterns of thought dominate our minds and experience that the old ways seem unconvincing and unsatisfying.

The time has come for serious rethinking. It is no longer enough to change a few words here and there in our prayers and hymns in order to make them more suitable; a more basic reorientation is called for. We need to recast our re-

ligious language and patterns to fit our new thought forms
and at the same time to preserve and enhance the values
that were won through the old concepts and attitudes. We
are not content simply to drop the old ways of praying. We
are searching and, to a rewarding extent, finding satisfying
new procedures that yield many of the values that have
always been associated with the practice of prayer. They
have the added value of being consistent with our total
philosophy.

Logically enough, our most fruitful experimentations to
date have been in finding new ways in prayer and worship
with the youngest children. But the need is pressing to experiment on the older age levels and with adults, also. What
are some of the new ways, and what values are being
achieved through them? Perhaps we can best answer these
questions against the backdrop of the old ways.

Traditionally, bedtime has been the time to listen to a
child's prayers. Remember Christopher Robin saying his
prayers?

> . . . Hush! Hush! Whisper who dares!
> Christopher Robin is saying his prayers.
>
> God bless Mummy. I know that's right.
> Wasn't it fun in the bath tonight?
> The cold's so cold, and the hot's so hot.
> Oh! God bless Daddy — I quite forgot.
>
> If I open my fingers a little bit more,
> I can see Nanny's dressing-gown on the door.
> It's a beautiful blue, but it hasn't a hood.
> Oh! God bless Nanny and make her good.
>
> Mine has a hood, and I lie in bed,
> And pull the hood, right over my head,
> And I shut my eyes, and I curl up small,
> And nobody knows that I'm there at all.
>
> Oh! Thank you, God, for a lovely day.
> And what was the other I had to say?
> I said "Bless Daddy," so what can it be?
> Oh! Now I remember it. God bless me.[1]

Does not the charm in this poem lie in the fact that the reader sees the discrepancy between the adult goal in the prayer time and the child's? Christopher Robin keeps getting off the track — namely, the "God bless" list — and lets his mind run on about the things that really matter to him, such as dressing-gowns. We would say, from our new perspective, that it is only then that he is *really* praying.

We would invite Christopher Robin to open his fingers even a little bit more — in fact, to get up off the floor and sit down on the bed beside Mother and Daddy and have a good visit. For, if we were to begin our list of the values traditionally derived from bedtime prayers that we wish to preserve, we would head it with the values gained from time spent recollecting the day in the company of a loved grownup. But we would give this companionship in a straightforward way, so that children are not tempted into the common subterfuge of "using the prayer time selfishly" — that is, just as a means of lengthening the going-to-bed process and keeping Mother and Dad with them a little longer. The usual device is to drag out the list of items one is thankful for to extravagant lengths or to enlarge the "God bless" list into something resembling the telephone book.

Why waste this precious time for the children or ourselves by forcing them into the maneuver of composing these lists, when we might be having a really good visit together? Let them share directly with Mother or Daddy — or, if need be, with baby sitter or maid — the thought, "Wasn't it fun in the bath tonight?" In so doing, we achieve the value of an honest relationship with our children and a frank acknowledgment with them of the real need that prompts them. What children really want at bedtime is not God's blessing on all their relatives or an itemized list of their own blessings, but a grownup's companionship before departing into that unknown and sometimes terrifying land of sleep.

It may be asked: Are any values lost if children share

this time directly with their parents rather than addressing themselves to an unseen power? Not only are no values lost, we believe, but many positive values are gained. The disadvantages, mentioned in the preceding chapter, that stem from a young child's necessary distortion and over-simplification of a personified concept of God are all avoided. "How can God hear everyone praying all over the world, Mummy? He must have enormous ears."

There is also the value of learning what is on the minds and hearts of our children. It is far better to learn these things directly rather than by "listening in," so to speak. Moreover, children are so often afraid and perhaps ashamed before this unknown Cosmic Person that many of the things that ought to come out at prayer time are kept behind locked lips.

As children are helped to stretch their minds and feelings in going-to-bed times shared with loving adults, they may actually feel the same values that many adults feel when they speak of communion with God. But we believe that this is best achieved by children when they reach deep into the context of their daily living, not when they are instructed to address themselves to a God outside of themselves. To use theological language, we would say we are encouraging children to bring the experiences of God that they have had during the day into their consciousness. In this sense, the kind of prayer time we are talking of takes place in the presence of God. But until children can verbalize about God without misunderstanding, we prefer not to use the word "God" about these times with them.

Because the traditional prayer form of talking to God is begun at the suggestion of grownups and is not, we believe, a natural form through which children would express their ideas and feelings, there soon comes an age at which many children question the whole procedure of praying. As young as four, children are reported to be a little restive under this pattern that has been imposed by adults. They cease to be docile and "cute" about evening prayers. Having gone through the age of inflexible ritualism around two and a half or three — when, in homes where traditional prayers were taught, the children very probably refused to go to bed *without* saying them — they now enter a stage of testing the grownups. They may try to see how silly they can be about prayers, or they may become very self-conscious about the listening adult, putting into their prayers what they think the adult would like to hear and omitting their real concerns. Sometimes they may just declare a rebellion and refuse to say their prayers any more. It is at this point that many parents discontinue bedtime prayers.

We read recently of one father who, when this happened, hit upon the idea of getting down on his knees beside the child and praying with her. This exhibition of adult humility on the part of the father was enough to overcome her objection and no doubt has some real religious values. We would hazard the guess that the novelty of this will probably wear off after a bit.

The fact is that prayer is something that children, in many Protestant homes, if given the freedom outgrow. This usually takes place in their early school years. A group of parents at a meeting in a rather orthodox church school were up in arms at the suggestion made by the kindergarten teacher that formal prayers and worship services be omitted from the Sunday morning kindergarten program. She felt that the children were too young to profit from them. When the parents protested vehemently, the teacher put a question to them: How many of those who also had older children prayed at home with these other children or knew that they prayed on their own?

These parents, a little embarrassed, admitted that in none of their homes was prayer practiced with the older children; all had stopped at about the first-grade level. The teacher suggested that this fact might be interpreted to indicate that there was something wrong with the way in which two- and three-year-olds are started in prayer. Our culture does not seem to support it as did earlier cultures. The practice of family prayers is very uncommon.

In a discussion of behavior patterns of a group of seven-year-olds, Gesell and Ilg report "less praying as the child takes on responsibility of own nighttime routines." [2] A young pastor in an orthodox church, who was teaching a class of junior-high boys, discovered that the subject of their curriculum for the next quarter was to be "The Prayer Life of Jesus"; the aim of the course was to enrich the prayer life of the students. On the opening Sunday of the quarter, he asked the boys how many of them prayed at home. The answer was: not one.

If prayer, as taught in the majority of modern homes to two- and three-year-olds, were felt by the children to be deeply satisfying, if it were really in touch with the children's needs and natural forms of expression, it would probably not die out when they were on their own; nor would it be discontinued by parents because of children's silliness or open rebellion. Something is amiss. Apparently the values that parents hope or believe are to be derived from the practice of prayer are not actually felt by the children.

We believe that prayer should not be introduced to children in such a way that they come to think of it as something for babies and small children and something for which they soon feel too big. A dominant idea that gets through to children given orthodox teaching is that prayer is a kind of magic. Many of these children, it has been found, believe that by their petitions they can obtain things that they want and cannot obtain in any other way. [3] Between the ages of six and ten, faith in this "kind of magic" is usually discarded along with Santa Claus — and very often God. Sometimes children give God a few crucial tests to pass before they finally give up their belief in the efficacy of prayer; in most cases He fails the tests, and that ends the children's attempts at prayer for a good many years, and sometimes for life.

The new ways of achieving the values won through prayer, we believe, make it possible to introduce the practice without introducing sham, disillusionment, and confusion. In an article on prayer, a minister described a conversation that he had had with a nine-year-old girl. The little girl in closing said, "I guess I understand part of what you're saying — but I'm still confused." "Well, you just stay confused," said the minister. "That's good, because when we're confused we do some thinking and sometimes by thinking we learn something." [4]

We question the necessity of growth through confusion. We have found that a more natural approach to prayer encourages children in genuine exploration, wondering, and discovery, but that no sense of confusion need be involved. It is usually because an anthropocentric theology has been taught or picked up from friends that the confusion arises. The children's actual experiences have no note of confusion. With a more natural approach, children will not outgrow prayer, but will grow into deeper and richer ways of reflecting on and evaluating their own living.

Liberal religious parents have experimented with new ways on the basis of what we know about children. For example, we know that for many years the wish for someone to tuck the child in at night and to sit down on the side of the bed for a chat is very real. We know that a child does not outgrow the enjoyment that comes from looking back over his days and years as part of a growing family. The fun of reading together, singing together, playing games together in the family — this is not outgrown in the pre-adolescent years.

In the third volume of the "Martin and Judy" books, the story called "The End of the Day" suggests a practice that

many of us experimenting in new ways in prayer have found
very meaningful.[5] Martin's mother writes down for him, in
a little notebook kept for this special purpose, the nicest thing
that has happened that day. One little boy called his book,
"My Fun Day to Remember," and decorated a cover for it.
Actually we have found it more releasing to suggest that it
is good to put down the not-so-fun things, too. Anything
can go into this book. Weeks may go by without any entries,
and then it may be called for every night for a while. "Want
to write in your thought book tonight?" might be an occa-
sional query.

Keeping such books (with a new one arriving in the
Christmas stocking each year) has many values. One value
is the perspective it gives even a young child on his still
brief life. Children love to have the books of past years
brought out and read from. They laugh at their primitive
story forms: "And then Daddy walked on the ice, and then
it cracked, and then Daddy fell through." They relive
some of the high spots: the first butterfly hatched, the first
kite flown ("weren't we dopes not to know not to bow a
kite!"), the day baby brother came home from the hospital,
the day mother accidentally set the backyard on fire. They
see how they have grown, how they have assimilated both
exhilarating and frightening events, and how, even in a few
years, their small worlds have changed and they have taken
it in their stride. Children of eight and nine may be ready
to keep records of their own, but they will still want to share
them with a grownup.

Reading over baby books kept by the parents, looking at
family picture albums or family movies, as described in the
story "Always Learning" in *Always Growing,* has many of
these same values.[6] With the smallest children, of two and
three, one of the most satisfying procedures is to retell the
events of a day in simple story form. Older children love to
be told stories of when they were younger or when their

parents were little.[7] These are all natural ways of achieving some of the values that prayers of thanksgiving and recollection have had down through the ages; these are ways in which children can participate naturally, joyously, meaningfully, without misunderstanding, deception, or embarrassment.

What about other kinds of prayers? Some research has been done on what children who are taught in traditional ways tend to pray for. According to an article written about this study, most parents reported that their children did not spontaneously pray prayers of repentance. Children did this only after adults suggested that they do it.[8] We agree that children do not spontaneously suggest that they would like to confess and be forgiven for something they have done. They do often yearn to get things off their chests, however, and it sometimes takes skill to help them bring themselves to talk about these things. They also need and respond to help in occasionally looking at and evaluating the kind of person they are becoming. Mutual acknowledgment of the needs and drives that children have at different times can make it possible for us to help them find satisfying and socially acceptable ways of living with these needs. Just because children do not naturally pray for forgiveness does not mean they really are completely happy about the way their lives are going.

According to the old ways of prayer, the child was urged to confess his wrongdoings and to ask God for forgiveness and for strength to be a better boy or girl. Perhaps one unhealthy reason parents have rather enjoyed hearing a child's bedtime prayers was that the parents seemed to get cosmic backing for the battles they had won during the day. God always seemed to be on the side of the grownups. He was another one of them — but even bigger and stronger. How much better for parents and children to sit down together and dig out the causes that lie behind whatever difficulties have come up during a day. Especially after a rough day (and what family doesn't have them?), we need to bring out into the open, if we can, the troubled feelings, the fears, the injustices that are gnawing at our hearts. More often than not it is the parents who cause the trouble; but how hard it is for us to admit it! How much easier to cast out the mote in our children's eye than the beam in our own! Things might proceed more smoothly if we could approach them with the question "Let's see what's going on here?" rather than "Who is to blame?"

But it is far easier to advocate bringing the causes of conflict and tension out into the open than to succeed in doing it. In one family time was always taken at bedtime, if not sooner, to discuss the causes of conflict. But one night the talk between mother and son only seemed to be adding fuel to the fire, augmenting the mother's angry feelings and the son's flow of tears.

Finally, in despair, the mother got up and said, "You'll have to go to bed now. We just can't get it straightened out this time." And downstairs she went. In a few minutes a couple of bare feet came pattering down the stairs, and the weepy little boy said very determinedly, "I've never gone to bed with mad feelings yet, and I'm not going to tonight. I know it would give me awful dreams." Mother was so impressed by his "faith" that she made one more determined effort, and everything was finally cleared up.

We parents cannot hope to be expert therapists, but we do need to acquire some techniques for successful talks with our children.[9] We need to be good listeners, to do less of the talking than we often feel we want to. We should try to treat our children with respect and handle discussions and decisions democratically. Perhaps we could do this more successfully if we were really convinced of what is in fact the case — namely, that we as much as the children are still growing and changing. We are all of us continually facing what, in the lingo of our day, are called "developmental tasks."[10]

It is recognized that many two-year-olds have certain basic needs and tasks, while seven-year-olds have others. But twenty-five-year-olds and thirty-five-year-olds do, too. We parents and teachers tend to think of ourselves as finished products and of children as imperfect items in the process of being formed. But a mother, for example, needs to be aware of the innumerable factors that influence her life and the way she handles her children: whether she was twenty or thirty-five when she had her first child, whether she has two children or six, whether her husband is succeeding or failing, and so on. Such matters vitally influence our relations with our children.[11] Adult living is a continual series of adjustments to changing factors. Unless we recognize this and are able to handle our reactions with some success, we tend to take out our failures, frustrations, and fears on the children we are dealing with.

If direct conversations with our children about some upset in the day only seems to augment tension, or if children seem unable to bring up things that we feel they would really like brought out into the open, there are other means that can be used. The stories in *The Tuckers: Growing to Know Themselves*[12] can serve as wonderful releasers and conversasation starters. They can also give a more objective character to some of the issues that arise in a day. There are other here-and-now stories that can be used for these purposes also.[13]

Dramatic play — acting out issues with mother playing son and son playing mother, or sister being little brother and little brother being bossy big sister — may bring real insight to everyone involved. We all need exercise in empathy, feeling what the other person feels so that we can understand what makes him "act that way."

Children spontaneously do this kind of thing. As young as two years old they begin to "make-believe." They play being Mommy, the milkman, the big dog at the corner — anything and everything that is a part of their real world. They want to understand this world, and they want to learn to live in it unafraid. For some first-graders it is almost a compulsion, the minute school lets out, to come home and play school. They must be the cross teacher, or the "bad boy" who upsets the class. Children achieve similar ends through play with dolls or puppets.

From observing groups of children we can learn effective non-verbal methods of meeting their need to bring their problems out into the open. Paint and clay are also good media through which children can communicate their concerns. Whatever means are chosen, the ends we seek are the same ends as have been traditionally sought through formal prayers of confession or prayers for strength.

One of the serious shortcomings of the old ways of prayers for forgiveness and strength lay in the fact that they encouraged in children the attitude that some mysterious force outside of them, working magically, could make them better boys and girls or free them from their fears. We wish to encourage in children an attitude that the causes of their thoughts and actions lie in the analyzable context of their daily lives. If change and improvement are to take place, this context must be looked at and dealt with realistically.

A little girl, aged six, asked her mother to teach her a prayer to say at night like her best friend, a Lutheran. The mother reports: "I urged her to make up her own prayer, and she said, 'One thing I'm going to pray for is a night without any bad dreams.'"

Now just to pray for no bad dreams seems to us a rather futile hope, since we know now fairly well the sources of our dreams. Would it not have been far more effective for this mother to have tried to uncover with the little girl possible causes for those dreams in her everyday living? As long as the causes of the trouble remained, we believe her prayers could not be answered. She asked from a real need; she deserved an answer that would bear fruit. To save our children from bad dreams takes more time and effort on our parts and theirs than a hurried prayer. These new ways of handling prayers with children take more skill, more humility, more sense of our own involvement in children's lives than the traditional way.

A grandmother reports this interesting episode. She took her three-year-old grandson Peter driving one day, and they passed a large airplane propeller mounted as a memorial to Amelia Earhart.

The little boy asked, "What's that?"

His grandmother attempted to explain. In the course of her explanation, she described the flier as "a nice lady, like Mummy." She told how something may have gone wrong with the lady's airplane, and how she had never been seen again. The grandmother had lost a flier son in the war, and Peter had been told at another time of how Uncle Ben had died.

The usual bedtime practice in this home was to tell the story of the little boy's day to him. On this particular night it was the grandmother's turn. She began the story of their day together, of the drive through the country, of the airplane propeller.

"No, no," broke in Peter excitedly, "not that."

The grandmother, amazed, skipped on to the next event. As she and Peter's mother talked the incident over, they decided that the reference to Amelia Earhart as "a nice lady, like Mummy," must have given the little boy the frightening thought that Mummy, too, could disappear and die. In various ways they hoped to work out this worry and help him handle this fear.

If this practice had not been part of the going-to-bed routine, Peter's unspoken prayer that Mummy would not die might never have been heard nor help given. Instead of telling children of "guardian angels 'round their beds," we want them to feel, if we can, that we stand ready to help them day and night.

Traditional religion has rather encouraged, implicitly if not explicitly, the idea that not knowing just how or why help came, either for a change in character or release from fear and despair, made it somehow more valuable and more religious. Theologians speak of the mystery of grace, unde-served help that comes from outside the person, giving him the extra push — or, rather, pull — needed to face reality and reorient himself. They speak of conversion, the seem-ingly miraculous about-face that transforms the "old" into the "new" man.

We feel that we must rid ourselves of the notion that not to understand clearly how something works makes it more "religious," more apt to be God-sent. Such an attitude en-courages the notion that faith and knowledge must clash. We believe that, the more human emotions are studied and understood, the greater will be the opportunity to cooperate by conscious planning with the forces of healing and growth in our Universe.

We want our children to know that there is help available: help that can come through parents and teachers aware of the laws that govern human emotions and human growth; health that can come through increased self-understanding. We need to keep ourselves and our children in touch with the health-giving and healing forces in the Universe. But we need to realize that growth that has been thwarted, forced into unhealthy and distorted patterns, is not freed without great effort. Many would say that the change that is ac-complished in a psychoanalysis is precisely this — the

planned break in the vicious circle of an unhealthy per-
sonality pattern.[14]

Another value that people have gained from traditional
ways in prayer has been the feeling that, having "taken it to
the Lord in prayer," they could trust Him. And yet, as
prayer is actually understood, or misunderstood, by children
and many adults, very often they find that this trust has been
misplaced. They become disappointed in Him and angry.
"It's hardest to believe in God when I ask for certain things
and don't get them. Then it's hard to think about Him
nicely."

The mother of five-year-old Mary tells this story. The
mother's sister, Mary's Aunt Jenny, was very sick. The
mother was in the habit of saying prayers at night with Mary.

One evening the little girl said, "Please Mummy, tell God
to make Aunt Jenny well."

The mother was pleased when Mary spontaneously said
this. The mother reported: "I was glad that she already felt
that there was Some One in the Universe whom she could
trust."

But Aunt Jenny did not get well. Aunt Jenny died.

"Why did God do that, Mummy?" asked Mary. "Why did
he let her die?" The mother commented later: "I did not
know how to answer that question."

Did this have to happen? What became of the attitude
of trust that this little child so confidently felt? Is this the
way to build a sturdy faith? Is this the best way to have
death faced, as a failure on God's part to do what was asked
of Him? Is God to be felt as trustworthy only if He does
what we ask?

We think the answer to all these questions is no. Nor is
Mary to be blamed for what she expected of God. The idea
of God which she had been taught, and the idea of what

can be effected through prayer, lay at the base of her difficulty.

What if Mary and her mother had prayed for Aunt Jenny
in a different way? They might have thought together of
all the forces at work helping Aunt Jenny. Instead of making
the little girl conceptualize a Big Force or Person that could
mysteriously or magically make Aunt Jenny well, the mother
could have talked to her about various specific and therefore
understandable healing forces already at work: the doctors
using all their skill, knowledge, and medicines; the nurses
watching her bed day and night; the healing powers in her
own body. The mother could have told Mary that she would
visit Aunt Jenny to show her love for her; and she might
have suggested that Mary could make a card to cheer her.
All these working together would strengthen Aunt Jenny.
But the mother could add very frankly that she did not know
whether these would be enough to make Aunt Jenny well.

When Aunt Jenny died, Mary would indeed be saddened.
She could be helped to see that Aunt Jenny had been too sick
to get well. But there would be no feeling on Mary's part
that *she*, Mary, had been betrayed. She could feel secure in
knowing that all they knew how to do had been done, and
that death is to be welcomed if a person is too sick to go on
living.

According to the mother's approach, which is a traditional
one, God had failed. For a reason Mary could not understand, He did not choose to save Aunt Jenny; the sense of
trusting God, on which her prayer was based, was destroyed.
Does not such a way of teaching children encourage imma-
turity and lessen their ability to face the real world? This
inability is one of the doors that opens into mental sickness.
Experience with death can be spiritually enriching, but
handled in this way it was spiritually impoverishing. We
have a responsibility to help children to a realistic awareness

of the sense in which it is valid to say, "Underneath are the everlasting Arms."

We can, indeed, put our trust in a variety of nature's manifestations: the rhythms that permeate nature; tides and seasons; cycles of growth and decay; the steady passage of the stars and planets in their appointed courses; the laws that govern physical and mental health holding sway within our very bodies. Bringing such phenomena into children's awareness through vital experience is the valid way to develop their feelings of living in a Universe that can be trusted.

Traditional ways of teaching children about prayer mislead them, because of the children's necessary literal-mindedness. In the book called *Tell Me About God*, a little boy asks his mother if it will be all right to ask God for a rabbit. The mother, having earlier assured the little boy that God is ready to listen to anything, reiterates this idea. "God will hear you, dear, whatever you talk about with Him. But often there may be reasons *that you do not know* why it is not good for you to have many things *that you think you want.*"[15]

This seems to us a cruel thing to tell a child. It certainly lessens his feeling of self-reliance as well as any warm feelings toward God. For a child it is unpleasant enough to have adults know what is good for him without assigning this characteristic to God too.

The little boy knows that if getting a rabbit is left up to Mummy and Daddy he won't get one; Daddy has told him that he may not have one until he can take care of it himself. Obviously the little boy hopes that God is stronger than his father and that he may stand a chance of getting a rabbit from God.

No wonder children mangle the concept of God and the idea of prayer until God takes on the character of a magician and prayer becomes a hope-against-hope kind of asking for things from this magician! Our modern world is full of people who have suffered inevitable disillusionment about the reality of this cosmic magician and the power of prayer to get them what they want. Many of these people have never taken the trouble to reconstruct their shattered faith; oddly enough, in a majority of cases they inflict the same traumatic experiences on their own children, for want of having given any real thought to the whole subject.

The little boy's wish for a rabbit is a subject that deserves the warm and sympathetic attention of his parents. They should discuss all the pros and cons with him, including the possibility that perhaps they will have to help take care of it for a while. At any rate, they should bring the subject to a close without letting the little boy think that, if Mummy and Daddy won't let him have a rabbit, maybe God will. One little girl, it was reported, figured out that God only gave you *things* you prayed for when you asked for them for *other people*.

Even this rationalization is finally shattered by reality, and by the end of their primary years most children have pretty well given up asking for *things* in their prayers. In a study made of what junior-age Protestant children pray for, weather and health were found to predominate — in other words, those forces before which children feel helpless.[16] Poor people and war are social phenomena of the kind that are also popularly wished away in prayer by children. But, all too soon, they discover that even these are too much for God. The question the child of orthodoxy must ask again and again is: Can I maintain my faith in God and prayer in *spite* of the evidence of my own experience?

We want our children to proceed in exactly the opposite direction, constructing a concept of God and an understanding of prayer out of their own vital experiences. The little boy who refused to go to bed with his mad feelings knew what he believed and knew what things pertained to his salvation. No one had taught him any words about God's wanting him to first make peace with his mother.

With a new approach to prayer there can be a freeing of it from a rigid association with bedtime and meals. We believe that there should be no division of life into sacred and secular, and, with the saints, we believe that an attitude of prayer can suffuse all of life. Even quiet talking times need not be just for bedtime; weeding the garden, mending clothes, drying dishes, rebuilding the chicken house, painting a room — all can be hallowed today as they were by Brother Lawrence and the saints through the ages.

Creative activities, mentioned earlier for their therapeutic values, also yield values that have been associated with appreciation and worship. Sketching, modeling, painting, dancing, dramatizing stories can all be used to carry our prayers. Writing letters as a group to persons far away can bring those persons closer in our thoughts and feelings. Asking mind-stretching questions, perhaps keeping books of questions for which we hope someday to know answers, can be a kind of prayer.

Reading poetry together is especially recommended for achieving the spiritual refreshment traditionally associated with prayer. Poetry is a form of expression for our feelings, and using it with our children will give them an early introduction to language used in a non-literal way. There is an increasing amount of poetry available that speaks to the hearts of children. The poems of Dorothy Aldis, for example, so many of which are very amusing, are thoroughly enjoyed by children.[17] Traditional religion has been such a humorless affair! Our new ways are ways that allow children to be honest and to show their real feelings, and we believe that genuineness and humor often go together. We can expect, then, that our new ways in prayer and worship will include many moments of hearty laughter.

We are still searching for adequate songs to sing in our new kinds of prayer times, but an increasing amount is becoming available.[18] The collection *Martin and Judy Songs* contains one of the most satisfying bedtime prayer-songs for little children:

> Now quietly I lay me down
> For day is gone, and night has come.
> Goodbye, sweet day! Goodbye, my play!
> I'm going to sleep in dreamland.
> I like the light. I like the night.
> Do you? Do you?

We should also encourage our children to compose their own songs and poems.

Perhaps one reason it has seemed so difficult to find adequate substitutes for the "great old hymns" is that so many of us have associated their use with the warm experiences of singing together in our childhood. The good feeling that was conveyed to us came in spite of the meaning of the words, which we often misunderstood or just didn't worry about. We hope the day will come when children can look back appreciatively not only on the happy occasions of having sung together, but also on the content of the songs themselves.

The old practice of reading together before bedtime is, of course, one of the finest ways of vicariously sharing experiences and extending horizons back in time and far in space. For the first ten years of children's lives, liberal religious parents should draw heavily on great books as a source of encouragement of spiritual growth with children. It is a kind of prayer, a communion, to experience life through the lives of others. By the age of ten, most children will fly the nest as far as most of their reading is concerned; so the early years are really the golden ones for entering with our children into the heritage of the past. It is an adventure to interpret with them the ideas and values that dominated different periods, and to find certain basic ideas and values appearing again and again in various cultures.

Probably in this age of television, children will cease being read to at an even earlier age, if they are read to at all. We as parents should make every effort to watch television often with our children, so that we may know what concepts and values are being thrust upon them. Unless children are given help in assimilating this material, they may be confused and spiritually impoverished.

We are confident that in more and more homes parents will find satisfying new ways in prayer with children. This will happen not as children kneel at our feet with heads bowed and eyes closed, but as we communicate together with "children's faces looking up, holding wonder like a cup."

10

Understanding Other Ways of Praying

"What were the men doing when they were spinning those wheels?"

There are certain very practical problems that liberal religious parents face as a result of experimenting with new ways in prayer. For one thing, some of the new ways that we may be substituting for the old ways are a far cry from what our children find in our culture labeled as prayer. As young as three or four, they will have witnessed formal grace said at meals, bedtime prayers at a friend's or cousin's home, or a congregation sitting with heads bowed in church. They may have watched television programs that suggest they must fold their hands and bow their heads before eating their crackers and juice. They may very possibly have been taught and be expected to participate in the Lord's Prayer in their public school. They may have heard detailed reports of the efficacy of traditional prayer.

Again, as with the idea of God, our children need ways of thinking and feeling about these traditional practices in which they are sometimes expected to participate, and which so obviously have social approval. They need help in relating what we are doing with them in our new ways to what others are doing in the traditional ways.

Our children's reactions may range from either of two extremes. On the one hand, some envy their orthodox friends with their set prayers. We believe that if liberal religious parents are really doing a good job and using vital new procedures, the children will themselves recognize how much more satisfying these are than set prayers. If a child asks for a prayer to say, it might be well for the parents to see if they can discover what values the child thinks this prayer will have, and then find deeper ways of satisfying this need.

At the other extreme will be children who are repulsed by the traditional ways and the pious attitudes of their play-mates or other adults. They may not even wish to relate this mysterious practice to something they so genuinely enjoy as their own bedtime routines or other kinds of prayer times. This is especially true when our children run up against an authoritarian display of orthodox practices, as is vividly dem-onstrated in this conversation between an eleven-year-old girl and her mother. (This occurred outside the United States.)

Dorothy: I hate Friday afternoons at school!

Mother: Why? What do you do on Fridays?

Dorothy: We have *religion* and I hate it! It's boring!

Mother: Why? You like Sunday school and can hardly wait for Sunday school to start. What are you studying about in religion in school?

Dorothy: Oh, Miss S. reads from the Bible and we talk about it, and then we have to say a prayer. It's awfully boring!

Mother: Some of the stories in the Bible are very interest-ing. What part of the Bible does Miss S. read?

Dorothy: Oh, any old place. I don't think she should. School isn't the place to have religion anyway — at least not what *she* calls religion!

Mother: What would you like to study on Fridays when you have religion?

Dorothy: Oh, religion can be interesting, but not *her* kind! She just reads and talks about "the Lord." It isn't interesting at all and besides, school isn't the place for that!

Mother: What is the place?

Dorothy: Well, people have a right to choose their own religion and their own church. They can have religion in their own Sunday school and talk about it in their own home. But at school Miss S. expects us to think the way she does. Religion isn't like arithmetic and spelling! There is only one right answer, and you're either right or wrong. But in religion, she has no right to try to make us think what *she* thinks. She can go to her own church, and so can all the children in the class. . . . I bet if she went to our Sunday school she would be shocked. She wouldn't even think we studied religion. . . . We learn about lots of different kinds of thinking and it's interesting — not like that boring "Lord" business she talks about all the time.

Mother: Probably people from other Sunday schools would think that the things we do in our Sunday school are queer. Maybe they would be bored with what we do.

Dorothy: Well, they might be surprised, but I bet they'd like it better. We have fun and *do* things. Of course, we talk about it, too, and sometimes we have discussions. But it is interesting, and it's all about what *I* call religion — how the world began, how things grow, and about the ways lots of different people think. What Miss S. calls religion is just what's in the Bible and it's boring — all that "Lord" business. "The Lord this" and "the Lord that" . . . and then the praying she makes us do!

Mother: What kind of praying?

Dorothy: Oh, a prayer she got out of some book. We are going to have to learn it, and every day when the bell rings we've got to bow our heads and fold our hands and say it. I hate that, too.

Mother: I thought you meant each child said a prayer or took turns.

Dorothy: No . . . we all have to say *her* prayer and ask God to forgive us and ask God for this and that. That's what she calls praying. I guess she'd say that I never did pray, and I don't if that's what you call praying. But I do think about things and what I've done and how I can improve on it and what I'd like to do. I just think these things out myself. Now what Miss S. calls praying is asking the Lord for this and that and not doing anything for yourself. I'd like it better if she just let us make up our own prayers. I think that's the only fair way to do it in school.

Mother: Well, I agree with you, but the school authorities have decided that all children should study religion in school. They have decided on what the teachers should teach, so I guess Miss S. has no choice.

Dorothy: If we had our kind of religion in school, it wouldn't bother anybody. At Sunday school Mr. M. doesn't try to make anyone in our class think just what he thinks, even though it is just a Unitarian Sunday school. And we talk about lots of different ways of thinking, not just one way. If we get bored, we paint or draw or make things in clay. But not in *our school!* We just have to sit and listen to Miss S. talk about what she thinks and answer her questions and pray for the bell to ring. Yes, that's what *we* pray for!

What can we do to prevent such an attitude as this from developing? Perhaps we should emphasize first of all, as we suggested with the word "God," that prayer is something different people have understood very differently. People have always expressed their prayers in a variety of ways.

A seven-year-old boy attended the movie *The Conquest of Everest.* After the movie he asked his mother, "What were the men doing when they were spinning those wheels?"

"They were praying," said his mother.

"No," the boy said. "I know how people look when they are praying. I mean the men who were pushing those drum things around."

"Those were prayer wheels," said his mother. "You see, people have very different ways of praying, and that is one way they pray in Nepal."

The sooner children are introduced to the idea that there are different ways of praying and different ideas about what one is doing when one prays, the better it will be. This will help perhaps to establish the idea that we have as much right to use the word "prayer" to describe what we are doing in our new ways as do their orthodox friends with their traditional forms.

Our second positive step, as with the idea of God, might be to attempt to relate the word "prayer" to the new ways in prayer in the child's own experience. This is what one mother did. Her little son, aged five, had been put to bed the previous night by a visiting grandmother.

"Grandma wanted to know if I say a prayer before I go to bed."

"Oh," replied his mother, "and what did you say?"

"I said no. She started to leave, and I told her that we always had a story or a talking time and a song. I asked her to tell me about when you were a little girl. Why did she want me to say a prayer?"

"Well," said Mother, "Grandmother thinks of God as a person to whom it is good to talk. I think of God more as the power in the world that helps us grow. It seems to me that mothers and daddies can work with this power more and help their boys and girls grow if they talk to their children about what's happened each day, and read with them at night, and things like that. That is the way I think of prayer. Perhaps when you're bigger your thoughts will be more like grandmother's, and then perhaps you'll want to use the kind of prayers she does."

"I like to talk to you and Daddy, Mum. Grandmother told me you used to have a goat — tell me about it."

When children bring home ideas about prayer that are essentially magical, or when they hear about prayer ways from primitive cultures, then we may want to try to relate these ideas and practices with a more primitive approach to reality, as we did with the idea of God. Our children will need to imagine a world of unpredictable and threatening forces amidst which men found they must learn to live without paralyzing fear. Somehow early man came to believe that all events were the results of the activities and whims of these forces which they personified as gods. Men did all they could to woo the gods. They pleaded with them in prayer, flattered them, praised them, thanked them, cooperated with them, and gave them the best they had in various forms of sacrifice. For these gods had wants and needs like human beings, and to please them it was wise to give them the best of the flocks or the crops; then, perhaps, they would leave unharmed the rest of a man's possessions.

In the book that we earlier suggested still needs to be written, *Beginnings of Faith and Worship*, we would like to see material gathered from primitive cultures all over the world, illustrating a variety of ways of prayer and worship. Children are interested to know that some people prayed by flying kites, some by making sand paintings, some by arranging feathers on a stick, some by painting pictures on the walls of caves, some by dancing and beating drums. It is extremely difficult for us really to know how early men thought, and what they believed they were accomplishing by their dances, rituals, and other ceremonials. Difficult as the task is, we believe the attempt should be made to understand this and interpret it to children.

The Caves of The Great Hunters, written for children nine and above, is a fascinating attempt to understand the thinking that may have been behind the cave paintings and carvings of prehistoric men.[1] *Waterless Mountain* is a magnificent attempt to make real the religious thought world of the Navajo Indians.[2] This can be read with children nine years old and over; the book can make a vital contribution to a child's understanding of a non-scientific approach to experience. Prayer plays a very large role in Navajo religious thinking.

Actually the traditional prayer ways of our contemporaries are in some ways closer in spirit to the prayer ways of primitives than to our experimental ways. Both primitives and contemporary traditionalists believe that supernatural powers control events and can be urged to step in and alter the natural course of things.

Until a generation or two ago, the idea of Providence was a powerful ruling concept in the thinking of most men and women in our culture. We may find the idea coming up a great deal in the reading we do with our children, especially reading concerned with frontier life. It is also a common thought in many of the most popular traditional hymns. At Thanksgiving we may try to interpret such hymns as:

> O God, beneath Thy guiding hand,
> Our exiled fathers crossed the sea. . . .
>
> We gather together to ask the Lord's blessing;
> He chastens and hastens his will to make known. . . .

It is rather fun to think with children about these old ideas and to give as sympathetic interpretations as possible.

Is all the good that happens the result of God's control and special intervention and all the evil the result of his chastising? Christian orthodoxy itself has never been quite agreed on the matter. Some thinkers have assigned the evil in the world to our human ignorance or inability to see the whole of the human drama; some have made the Devil or other evil spirits the chief cause. Others have believed that evil was God's punishment on wicked men, while still others assign the responsibility for evil to several causes, one of the chief being man's sinful heart.

But there has been rather universal agreement that, wherever the burden of evil should fall, the credit for the good that comes to us belongs to God. After a recent New England hurricane an appeal for funds for victims was made on large prominently displayed posters. They read: "God Spared You. Give." Sarah, a seven-year-old girl, who laboriously worked out the words, asked her mother what they meant.

"Well," said the mother, "the person who wrote that sign believed that God watches over and protects people. 'Spared' means saved. That person believes that God saved us in this town from the hurricane, and therefore we should feel so thankful that we want to give money and clothes and things to the people that lost theirs."

"Why didn't God save the other people, too?" asked Sarah.

"Some people who think that way about God would say we just don't know why he saves some and not others. Other people would say God makes hurricanes to punish people who have been bad. I don't think of God that way myself."

"I'd hate that kind of God," said the little girl. "And that isn't how a hurricane gets made anyway. Daddy showed me a weather map, and that showed how the hurricane got made."

"Do you remember the book we read about the Indian massacre in Deerfield?" asked her mother.

"Yes," said Sarah.

"Remember how the people who didn't get killed kept thanking God for having saved them and for having protected them? This is that idea we talked about then — the idea of Providence, God taking care of people. It's an idea people have often had when they lived not knowing whether or not they would be alive tomorrow. We feel differently about it, partly because we can tell a little better what is going to happen and what to expect. We don't have hurricanes very often, and some of these old ideas come up almost without our thinking, when we're in sudden danger.

"Men in wars sometimes have this idea, too, when they know there isn't much they can do about whether or not they will be shot. They think, 'Well, if God is taking care of me, I'll live, if He isn't I'll die.' It seems to help them not to worry."

Another mother, who also felt a need to make the idea of Providence understandable, took her children, nine and seven, through an old graveyard. This was something they always were interested in doing. They stopped before some of the oldest gravestones and read the names and epitaphs. They noticed how many graves were those of little children.

" 'Azariah Swett, age 91.' Well, he had a good long life," said the nine-year-old philosophically.

" 'Elizabeth Adams, born January 9th, 1802, died January 11th, 1802. Only a bud, destined to bloom in a better land,' " read the mother.

"Golly, only two days old," said the seven-year-old. "What's that mean about the bud, Mummy?"

As the mother began to explain, the nine-year-old said, "Oh, look, this one is 'Sarah Adams, mother of Elizabeth, died January 9th, 1802.' She must have died having the baby. I'm glad we didn't live then, Mummy. I wouldn't want you to die."

"Yes," said the mother. "Before there were shots and vaccinations and all those things, a lot of babies and mothers and children died. People needed ideas like Providence and Heaven to keep them from feeling too sad. They thanked God when they lived, and yet they didn't usually get mad at Him when their children or wives died. I wonder why that was? I wonder how I would have felt?"

It is interesting to point out to children that other religious systems have had other large ideas that help their members face life's crises. In the East, for instance, the belief in continuous rounds of incarnations helps those who are very poor or very unfortunate to tolerate their existence, hoping for a better lot in their next incarnation. When children are older they will want to evaluate these large ideas, testing them for their truth and adequacy.[3] What ideas will sustain us in the face of atomic disaster? Should we search for such ideas, or just take reality as it comes?

In our attempt to help our children understand the prayer ways of others, we have one very practical problem for which there is no easy solution. In some parts of the country the children in the public schools are taught the Lord's Prayer and expected to say it daily. Since we believe that children ought not to repeat things that have no meaning for them, most of us make the attempt to explain this prayer so that it can mean something.

If you have never tried it, sit down with a six-year-old and see how much meaning — let alone spiritually enriching meaning — can be wrested from this prayer for him.[4] It is possible to explain what most of the phrases may have meant to Jesus, although the importance of such concepts as God's kingdom and the forgiveness of sins lie outside the realm of a child's experience. But the prayer just isn't very interesting or very vital to a child under ten. It certainly does not express his deep needs and real feelings. If our children repeat it, we do not think they are praying as we understand prayer.

Secondly, even if your children will let you go through the prayer, phrase by phrase, clarifying meanings, the problem still remains of what to do about the fact that children must repeat it day after day. Very soon, as with most people, they will pay lip service to the prayer, while their minds are far away. This is precisely the attitude toward prayer and religion that we do not want to encourage in children. We do not want religion to be something you do but don't think about.

Some of our children may rather enjoy being able to say the Lord's Prayer. They sense perhaps that it is forbidden fruit at home. And being able to say it makes them more like their friends, which they desire. But the novelty of this will wear off.

One little girl in the first grade told her mother that they said the Lord's Prayer every day at school.

"Oh," said her mother, "did the teacher explain what it means?"

"No," said the little girl, "but I almost know it."

"Do you know what Jesus told his friends before he told them that prayer?" asked her mother.

"No. What?"

"He said that one of the most important things not to do when you pray is to say the same prayers over and over as if the number of times you said something would make it happen. In many cultures people have believed that was a good way to pray. Jesus said God knows what you need before you even open your mouth. And yet that prayer of his is said over and over again by people. Some churches teach that the more times you say it the better God likes it. And yet that was just what Jesus believed you shouldn't do."

Another practical situation when children wonder what to do or think is when they participate in adult worship services or formal grace. Our concern is for the integrity of their feelings. We hope that children will develop a capacity for meditation and quiet wondering. We think it will develop, not by having it imposed from outside, but either as a genuine reaction to something they have felt deeply or when they are recollecting such times of deep feeling with parents or under the guidance of a skilled leader of worship.

This is probably at the base of the conflict we religious liberals feel in the use of rituals and set services of worship. We want the feelings and thoughts expressed in the worship to be genuine expressions of our own real feelings and thoughts; yet, so often when participating in worship services, we sense that if the prophet Isaiah or Jesus himself were present, he would rise up and cry out, "This people honors me with their lips, but their heart is far away from me." This is a problem that needs analysis by liberal thinkers.[5] We feel the dilemma even more acutely when children are forced to bow their heads and fold their hands to words and forms that we know find no response in their hearts.

In one home, instead of formal graces, the family often played games at meals that stretched their minds and feelings about the miracle of living and eating. In one game, they thought of where all the items in a meal had come from, or of all the animals that had contributed to the meal, or of all the people involved in producing it.

One day they had a young visitor, Harry, to lunch. When they sat down he asked if he might say grace before the meal. The rest of the group bowed their heads as Harry ran, very rapidly, through a traditional grace. Then, for the rest of the meal the guest acted rudely, monopolized the conversation, criticized the food, and generally made the meal unpleasant.

After he had left, the mother in the family asked the children how they thought the meal had gone.

"Harry was certainly a mess," said the seven-year-old son, who had entered right into the messiness with him!

"What was it he said in that grace?" asked the nine-year-old son. "I couldn't understand any of it."

"Many people have always said a prayer before they begin to eat," answered the mother. "The idea is that when saying grace they stop to think of all the wonders that have to do with food; of where the food has come from, of how it becomes a part of us, of all who have worked to bring it to us. Some people feel that it is only because God is taking care of them that they have food to eat and clothes to wear. It is good to stop and think about these things, but I'm not sure Harry's grace helped us to do that."

Some families have found simple and meaningful words that can be used again and again without becoming stereotyped and stale, and we all need to experiment further in this direction. Our only desire is that our children and ourselves shall express with our lips what we actually feel in our hearts.

We want to encourage our children to approach the prayer ways of others in an inquiring spirit. In this way we can make both our own religious quest and our differences with various orthodoxies occasions for rich thinking, rather than sources of antagonism. We are still at the threshold of discovery about the practice of prayer. We need to adventure much further before we can speak with certainty.

11

Interpreting Teachings About Jesus

"Does Marshall have a little friend named Jesus?"

In our culture, an awareness that there was a person named Jesus comes very early. Reports about Jesus begin to get through to children as young as three, and often in a very confused form.

The Jesus about whom young children first hear is usually the baby Jesus, at whose birth angels sang and kings knelt. Children are intrigued by the Christmas story, and if there is a baby in the house they will probably drape their heads with a scarf to play Mary, and roll the baby in a towel as Jesus.

Or our children may hear about a little boy named Jesus.

"Mother, does Marshall have a little friend named Jesus?" asked four-year-old Jean.

"Why, dear?" asked Jean's mother. "Why do you ask that?"

"Because he talks about a little boy Jesus and I don't know him."

"Perhaps," said Jean's mother, "Marshall is learning something about what we call history. History is the story of the long-ago time. Jesus lived long ago. We remember his birthday at Christmas because he was such a fine man. Perhaps someone told Marshall a story about what they thought Jesus was like when he was a little boy."

Some children bring reports of an adult Jesus who could do magic. That this adult is the same person as the baby or little boy is not always clear. Their friends may be thor-

136

oughly mixed up as to how to differentiate between God and Jesus, who seem to be the same — only somehow different.

Or, again, our children hear of Jesus who loved little children. They may hear him described as "the man in the dress," and they may sing that favorite song, with its catchy tune:

> Jesus loves me, this I know,
> For the Bible tells me so;
> Little ones to Him belong,
> They are weak but He is strong.

This Jesus was so kind and good that he was never cross and tired. Yet, paradoxically enough, he was killed. Children are very much interested in the stories they hear about his death and resurrection. They may want to know just where the nails went through his hands, and how he could have been walking around after he was dead.

If our children are growing up in a religiously conservative area, they may bring very bewildering questions about Jesus who should somehow be in their hearts, who washes their sins away, or who died for them. This Jesus we recognize as the main character in the Old Story of Salvation.

Many of us feel that a study of the life of Jesus is an important part of the religious education of our children. But we also believe that a serious study of his life is a difficult undertaking and should not come until the junior or senior high-school years. Believing this we are confronted with a very practical problem. What should we do in the intervening years, between approximately six and ten, as a very confused picture of Jesus is built up in our children's minds by the surrounding culture?

There are several constructive steps that liberal religious parents may take. For one thing, we may seek to establish clearly the fact that Jesus was a real man, whose life we hope they will study when they are older.

In the first "Martin and Judy" volume, written for three-year-olds, Christmas is described as the birthday of Jesus, a man who lived and died long ago.[1] As children begin to distinguish in their minds what can really happen from what we just pretend can happen, we will want to emphasize that Jesus was a real person about whom some just-pretend stories were made up.

It is unfortunately all too easy for children in our culture to think of Jesus as unreal or make-believe. Not only do they hear the Christmas legends about his birth, but at the same time they hear the Santa Claus myth. Very naturally these stories may all be lumped together in their minds. In the story "Christmas Together at Church," in *Always Growing*, a book for six- and seven-year-olds, the distinction is made between Jesus, who was a real person, and Santa Claus, who is a make-believe person.[2] The story suggests that it is easy for us to get mixed up about Jesus because of all the make-believe about angels and wise men, but that Jesus was once a real man.

Because we are seeking to establish in children's minds a picture of Jesus as a real man of long ago, perhaps we should stop here to evaluate the increasingly popular practice of telling young children stories about when Jesus was a little boy. Such stories are thought to have value by two quite different groups, with rather different motives.

Some holding quite orthodox views about the person of Jesus believe that this is an effective way of convincing children that Jesus was a real man as well as really God. They have listened to psychologists and educators, as well as theologians. The theologians have said: The life of Jesus must be taught as early as possible in order that children may know God as revealed through Jesus. The educators and psychologists have said: For children younger than seven or eight, Jesus can be made real and interesting only as he is shown as a real little boy, interested in much the same things as other children are.

A second group that welcomes this approach comes from among religious liberals. Is not this, they ask, a good way to introduce Jesus to our children? Surely it is better than the myths about his birth that intrigue children but that we don't believe, or stories about the adult Jesus that children can't understand and that are full of miracles. These parents and teachers report that their children hear about Jesus from their friends; these adults want to balance what the children hear with something liberal. They say: If we tell them what a real little boy in Nazareth was probably like, then they'll know he was real and not make-believe. There are now many books that portray Jesus as a real little boy. *Once There Was a Little Boy* by Dorothy Kunhardt is perhaps the best known and most widely used.[3]

We question, however, whether this is the soundest way to handle the problem. It gives children a familiarity with the name of Jesus, but little idea of why he was important. In many of these books, Jesus remains a little boy throughout the entire story, rather than growing up to manhood. This is done to hold the interest of the six-year-olds, but it contributes almost nothing to their grasp of the Jesus of history and may fix Jesus in their minds as a six-year-old. In so far as he is interesting to them, it is because they are able to identify with him; but usually he is pictured as so good, helpful, and kind that the six-year-old reader is a little repulsed. This is precisely the attitude that we do not want children to develop.

We do not provide six-year-olds with stories about what Socrates was like at six, or St. Paul, or Shakespeare, or Martin Luther. To do it with Jesus just to familiarize children with his name, or to correct a false picture, results in a further blurring of the historic figure, which is blurred enough without our adding to the confusion. We think it is desirable to avoid making Jesus a familiar character to young children, since they may become thoroughly bored by him before they have met the historic man at all. One mother who had used such books with her son reported that, at nine, "he thinks he knows all there is to know about Jesus, although he actually knows almost nothing yet about the historic Jesus."

Actually, of course, the childhood of Jesus is almost completely unknown; the stories must be fictitious. Although the stories are given as authentic a geographic setting as possible, they are usually put in a twentieth-century psychological setting. The authors probably feel that if the thought world is made too strange, it will be a barrier between Jesus and the modern six-year-old. As a result, the parents of Jesus are sometimes made to sound like contemporary American middle-class parents who are trying to handle Jesus with insight straight out of Gesell.

Liberal religious parents would perhaps be on firmer ground if they sought to present Jesus primarily as an *adult*. This does not mean that we must somehow stop up children's ears so that they won't hear the Christmas stories. Rather it means that we can let children enjoy these stories for what they are — wonder stories or legends woven around this real *man* as a way of glorifying him. Just as artists put halos around heads to set people off as special, writers weave stories like these. What possible reasons could we give to explain why the Christmas stories should have been written about a perfectly normal six-year-old Palestinian boy, just like our own children?

Actually, liberal religious parents and teachers who consistently emphasize Jesus as an adult figure are able to feel less on the defensive about Christmas; for they find it is not difficult to show children how legends have grown up and symbols have been used to enhance the figure of the historic Jesus.

Since our children cannot escape hearing the wonder stories of Jesus' birth, let us go out of our way to see to it that they hear stories of the miraculous births of other great men at the same time. In *From Long Ago and Many Lands* the three birth stories that bring together the legends that have gathered around the births of Jesus, Buddha, and Confucius are of inestimable value.[4] If parents and teachers will be sure to read pages 176 and 177 in *From Long Ago and Many Lands* for the point of view behind the presentation of these stories, they can then use as little or as much of them with their own children as they feel is needed. Reading these stories in this comparative setting demonstrates clearly that, because of the human need to express in poetic form our feelings about great men, the same treatment has been given the birth of all three teachers, each from very different cultures. At the end of each account of the birth stories there is a short statement about the kind of people these men really grew up to be. This helps children relate the stories to the real historic figures.

It is important to emphasize continually that all three were real men; although now we might want to express our feelings about a great person in other picture language than angels and wise men, this is how these earlier people were able to say, "Here is greatness." We might explore with children legends that have sprung up about the birth of more recent legendary heroes — Davy Crockett, with a cradle made from a snapping turtle's shell; Paul Bunyan, who was so huge at birth that he slept in an ox-cart; John Henry, born with a hammer in his hand.

We will want to tell our children that some people — many of their friends, perhaps — have been taught to think that these stories about Jesus' birth really happened; but we think they are like poems or pictures or stories that can have a truth in them and yet not be something that really happened. This distinction between having something true in it and being a true story is an interesting one to develop with children. There are many stories in the collection *From Long Ago and Many Lands* that are not literally true but that "hit home" with children. One of the most interesting to discuss and analyze for this purpose is "The Visit to the Land of Great Men." To discuss it with a six-year-old, an eight-year-old, and a ten-year-old is to see how the ability to think abstractly and non-literally develops.

There is an added value that comes from putting the birth story of Jesus in a comparative setting. It means that, from the first, our children will approach this figure as *one* great figure alongside others in the religions of the world. As our world continues to shrink, we are glad to think that our children may be in the forefront of those ready to celebrate the births and lives and insights of truth-seekers the world over, not blurring their different contributions nor narrowly and ignorantly exalting one above the other, especially when the others are not even known.

A little boy of six, with whom this approach had been used, once went into the chapel of an orthodox Sunday school with his mother. He saw a big cross up in front of the room.

"What is that for?" he asked.

"This is where the children think and study about Jesus, and that cross is to help them remember him."

"Do they study about Buddha, too?" he asked matter-of-factly.

Not only does the birth story of Jesus demonstrate the universal human tendency to exalt and create legends about the life of a great man, but it also demonstrates how the human mind works with symbols. Phenomena of birth and light very naturally lend themselves to symbolic use, as these birth stories illustrate. Using the children's own experiences, we can lead them into an understanding of ideas used symbolically.

If, for example, a family is living close enough to nature to be aware of the time of the rising and setting of the sun, children as young as five and six in the temperate zone realize the shortness of daylight hours near Christmas. Then comes, with remarkable swiftness, an increase in the daylight during the last week of December and the first week of January. One family kept a record, the father in his city office, the family at home, of the date on which they first noticed increased daylight in the afternoon. For two consecutive years the report was made simultaneously from the office and from home on January 7th.

Building on such actual experiences, we can help children see that the winter solstice is a natural time — and has always been a natural time — to rejoice at light coming into the world, the rebirth of the sun. How wise of the early church fathers to decide to celebrate the birth of Jesus at a time of natural celebration.

Can the children understand how a teacher might be called a "light"? If we are trying to understand something that is too hard for us, we may say, "We're in the dark." If a teacher comes along and helps us to understand how to do something, we may say, "The light dawned." The darkness of our ignorance is lighted up. Some people feel that way about Jesus' teaching. Others have felt it about other teachers. The name Buddha means "the man with the light." The Jewish festival of Hanukkah, celebrated at the same time of year, likewise uses the symbolism of light. There are numerous other examples.

We like to emphasize, too, not only that the birth of Jesus, or of Buddha, or of Confucius was like a light coming into the world, but that every baby who is born is a light that lights up the hearts of all the people around it. Christmas can be lifted beyond the particular birth of Jesus by relating

it to nature, to other births of wise and famous men, and —
what is most important to young children — to the birth of
real babies in the world around them. Religious liberals
might work on ways of celebrating Christmas as a day to
honor all the new babies born in a church each year.

An interesting conversation is reported in *Books Before
Five,* a diary record of Dorothy White's reading with her
young daughter. Mother and daughter had been looking at
the Petersham's book, *The Christ Child.*[5] The mother apparently holds an orthodox religious point of view about
Jesus.

Child: You said Jesus was a very special kind of baby?
Mother: He is.
Child: More special than Vicky? (*Her baby sister.*)
Mother: Well, yes, he is really. He is special to more people.
Child: (*Obviously trying to get to the nub of the situa-
          tion.*) But Vicky is the most special baby of all in
          the wide world — to us, isn't she? More special to
          us?

Mrs. White comments: "And I said she was. Unsound
theology, perhaps, but sound family doctrine."[6]

We disagree with this mother, since we feel that the sound
family doctrine *is* the child's theology and that it is sound
theology. But we would go on to interpret the adult theology
that the child was confronting in some such way as this:
Jesus was not more special when he was a baby than any
other baby, but when he grew up he was a specially fine man.
The people who loved him thought he was so good that he
must have been more than an ordinary person, even a God.
If he was so special, amazing things must have happened
when he was born, they thought; and these are the stories
they imagined.

Telling these birth stories is not the most important part of the religious education of the youngest children. When we use these stories with children as young as five, we do it as a kind of preventative against their taking literally the inescapable Christmas story. We doubt whether the symbolism of light and birth as presented in the stories can really feed the spirits of children under eight very much. Children, like the human race, emerge slowly from literal-mindedness. This literal-mindedness is familiar to any parent who lives closely with children. One mother remembers the horrified expression that came over the face of her five-year-old son, when she said casually to her husband, "Oh, I just lost my head, that was all." Hastily she added, "That's just an expression."

We find that children are confused, not only by the legendary birth stories and the fictitious stories about Jesus as a little boy, but also by the remarks of their friends who equate Jesus with God. Five-year-old Nancy listened wide-eyed as a little friend pointed to Jesus in the manger of a crêche. "See," said the friend, "there is God."

The following conversation was reported between two seven-year-old girls and a five-year-old boy.

"You know how Jesus made the first people?" asked seven-year-old Barbara. "He made mud people first, and then he made them alive."

"Hello, mud pie," said the five-year-old.

"Not any more, though," continued Barbara, apparently thinking on her own. "He just did that before. Now he makes babies."

"There were people alive before Jesus," challenged seven-year-old Brenda.

"Yes," said the five-year-old. "Joseph and his twelve brothers were alive."

"And Mary was alive, too," said Brenda.

"And the Egyptians," said the five-year-old, all excited, still thinking of the Joseph story he had once heard. "There were lots and lots of Egyptians."

And this conversation took place in a group of eight-year-old children in a church school.

"Well, God isn't a person," Philip said. "He's a great energy back of all the world, or a spirit if you want to call it that, but he isn't a person."

"Yes, He is a person because He came to the world," James said.

"No, He didn't," answered Philip. "You are thinking of Jesus."

"Well, they are the same," said James.

"Oh, no," said Philip. "Jesus was a man that lived and he came to the world, but God is the energy back of everything. He isn't a person, I tell you."

"Why, don't you see, James?" said Jean. "Jesus was a baby born just like all of us, and he lived in the world and died just like any of us. But God is something different." [7]

Our children will meet their Barbaras and their Jameses, too. We want to be sure that they have their facts straight before we try to interpret for them what seems like the utter confusion of their friends. Jesus was a man who was born, lived, and died. When they are older they will study about his life. Some people who knew him and other people who have read about him in the Bible have believed he was a very special man. Indeed they have thought he was so good he was really a god. Or others have said he was so good, that God must have been his father. Really, his father was Joseph.

The opening story in *From Long Ago and Many Lands,* "The Picture on the Kitchen Wall," is an excellent presentation of the way in which a good man gradually may have come to be thought of as a god. This story can be used satisfactorily with some five- and six-year-olds. It may help interpret to children how people have come to have this idea about Jesus. Because this story gives an example from the Chinese culture, it helps children see that to have thought this about Jesus is not unique. They can understand that it is a way people the world over have thought about great and good men, or about people with great power over other men.

It is in relation to the idea of Jesus as a god that we might look at the problem of Jesus' miracles. Seven-year-old Harry remarked to his mother, "Jimmy said that if Jesus were alive now he could just touch him and he'd be all well, and then the doctor wouldn't have to give him a penicillin shot. Nobody could do magic like that really, could they, Mother?"

"Well," replied Harry's mother, "I think I know how Jimmy may have gotten that idea. The Bible does have some stories in it that tell about Jesus' making sick people well. In one he just touched a woman, the story says, and she was well. People explained things very differently when Jesus lived than most of us do now. We don't understand exactly what did happen that made men write those stories."

Having said this, Harry's mother then tried to distinguish in her own mind the kinds of miraculous cures attributed to Jesus. She tried to interpret her findings to Harry.

For one thing, the people who lived at the time of Jesus believed that sickness was caused by evil spirits that got inside of people. Many early people have believed that. If the spirits could be made to leave the person he would be well. A person who could make them leave was supposed to have special power in him from God. Jesus probably believed this, too. We think of sickness differently now; some kinds we know are caused by germs or virus, and we have medicines that help us get rid of these sicknesses. We don't think Jesus could have cured people with that kind of sickness just by touching them.

But there are other kinds of sickness, caused largely by

our own feelings, and an understanding friend or doctor can help us get well from these. People have sometimes even been blind and deaf only because they were so afraid. Jesus may have been the kind of person who made people feel less afraid when they were with him. Thus he made them well. Children as young as six can begin to understand the idea of psychosomatic sickness. They may have a friend who always gets sick Monday morning on the school bus. He may actually be sick to his stomach, and yet the real seat of the illness is the thought of a week of school ahead.

In *From Long Ago and Many Lands,* "The Two Friends" is a story through which a discussion of this kind of sickness can be started with children of primary age. The account of Jesus curing Hannah in *Jesus the Carpenter's Son* might be discussed with nine- or ten-year-olds as a way of understanding how some of the cures attributed to Jesus might be reinterpreted. [8]

But the gospels also tell that Jesus made the dead rise. We believe that this kind of miracle isn't possible and that this would belong in the class of legends imagined to enhance the stature of Jesus. Instead of stating dogmatically that we think certain miracles just couldn't happen, it might be better to encourage young people to figure out what would be implied about our world if such miracles could happen. Does it seem to be that kind of world? If not, what reasons can we find for the accounts of miracles in the New Testament records? What big wishes, which all people have, lie behind some of these stories, just as they do in the miracles assigned to the heroes in familiar tall tales? We have found that this kind of frank and honest attempt to understand miracle stories is appreciated by children.

A good many other questions our children ask about Jesus can best be handled by relating them to the Old Story of Salvation, in which the historic Jesus is transformed into the symbolic Savior. This is especially true for children who are in contact with Roman Catholic doctrine or Protestant fundamentalism. Because our children will hear the story piecemeal from their playmates and through various media in our culture, we may find it valuable from time to time to tell them the main outline of this story.[9] An awareness of the whole story makes more understandable the many isolated references to it in our culture. This problem will be treated further in the next chapter, which discusses the Bible as a whole.

Many parents and teachers find that the practical situation demands that they give their children, especially those between six and ten, a certain amount of information about the content of Jesus' teaching and some of the historic events of his life.

"Why can't a good biography of Jesus be written for the nine- and ten-year-olds?" is a question that is frequently asked. We know that children of nine and ten are already avid readers of biography. The tremendous popularity of such series as the "Childhood of Famous Americans" and the "Landmark Books" testifies to this.

Unfortunately, as pointed out earlier, the childhood and youth of Jesus, which might interest nine- and ten-year-olds, is a blank on the pages of history. As for Jesus' adult life, until its dramatic ending, very little happened that would hold the interest of young readers. Jesus' life centered largely around ideas; in order to understand the little dramatic action that occurs, an understanding of these ideas is called for.

To further complicate things, we are not certain what some of the key ideas meant, either to Jesus or his contemporaries. Concepts such as the Messiah, the Kingdom of God, the Son of Man are not easily understood even by adults and scholars. It is for these reasons, we believe, that any biography of Jesus that tries to be true to history cannot be written for children under twelve. Either it will over-simplify and distort his ideas, or, if it seeks to present them accurately, it will necessarily bore children.

Since this is the case, we suggest that liberal religious parents and teachers should themselves become as well informed as possible about Jesus. Instead of just adopting and handing on uncritically the usual liberal evaluation of Jesus, each of us might well try to make our own fresh appraisal of the kind of person Jesus actually was.

This is not an easy task, but it is one that might yield many values. All through the history of the Christian Church, startlingly fresh developments have occurred when people have put aside second-hand evaluations of Jesus, have picked up the Bible, and have read for themselves the four gospels. Divesting ourselves of our liberal prejudices, as much as we can, we should read and see what picture of Jesus emerges for us from these records.

We realize that the picture of Jesus in the gospels is Jesus as he was understood by the persons who wrote these accounts. This picture depends, in part, on what Jesus actually was like and, in part, on the hopes and beliefs of the writers and editors of the records. These records were not written down until between thirty and a hundred years after Jesus' death, by men who probably themselves never knew Jesus. They were written by men who knew how Jesus' life actually ended and what happened to his followers in the years immediately after his death.

In this study we may want to use a "harmony" of the gospels — a book in which the three gospels that have basically similar material in them are arranged side by side.[10] This makes it possible to compare the records with each other. Why did later authors change earlier accounts, omit some material, add other material? We will need to consult encyclopedias and commentaries for necessary background

material about the period.[11] Unless we do this, our reading
will be naive. Our aim should be to discover behind these
records the historical Jesus.

This kind of study is carried on in nearly every first-rate
Christian theological seminary, as men prepare to become
ministers. If a group of parents or teachers find such a study
too difficult to do on their own, they could plan to meet with
a minister. They might be better able with his help to become aware of the questions that the Bible texts should
force them to ask.[12]

The results of such a study are not clear-cut. The kind of
person Jesus was is certainly not crystal-clear, nor are the
actual meanings of his teachings beyond dispute. The figure
of Jesus that emerges from a study of the four gospels is very
blurred; indeed, it would be more accurate to speak of the
figures that emerge, for it is extremely difficult to find one
coherent portrait of Jesus in these records. Although we
cannot, nor need we, know the answers to all critical problems before we attempt to deal with our children's questions
about Jesus, at least we should realize that such problems
exist.

Liberal religious parents and teachers might also find it
enlightening to read both *Jesus the Carpenter's Son* by Sophia Fahs, written for twelve- to sixteen-year-olds, and *Men
Called Him Master* by Elwyn Allen Smith, written for twelve-
to-fourteen-year-olds.[13] The former book presents Jesus, the
great teacher, constructed from Biblical records and a liberal
religious imagination. The latter book presents Jesus, the
incarnation of God, constructed from Biblical records and an
intellectual orthodox imagination. The two portraits of Jesus
are strikingly dissimilar. To read these books side by side
can give some awareness of where there is agreement about
the historic Jesus and what some of the major areas of dis-
agreement are. Such an awareness may help us be more

sympathetic toward the variety of opinions that exist on the subject of when and what to teach children about Jesus.

When we face the practical necessity of giving some information about Jesus' life and teachings to children under twelve, we must do so with all the skill we can. We will soon sense what children get out of our explanations, what slips over their heads, and when we have lost our audience!

"Mrs. Green said that I was a Good Samaritan today. What's that?" asked seven-year-old Betsy.

"Well, I'll read you the story of the Good Samaritan," said her mother, "and you see if you can tell me why she thought you were like him."

This mother reports: "I was amazed to discover that the only idea that my child got from this story was that a Good Samaritan is someone who helps people. All the subtleties that make the story great went right over her head. She didn't know that the priest and Levite were hypocrites. She admitted frankly that she might have hurried past, too. The child only felt the reality of being scared by the robbers, and though the people who didn't help were mean, their action was understandable. But the hypocrisy of the priest and the large-mindedness of the Samaritan were not real to her because of her immature grasp of the subtleties of social relations past and present. I was disappointed. I thought this was one story of Jesus that she could understand."

Many parents have had a similar experience with the story of the Prodigal Son. Jesus' teachings were concerned so much with adult attitudes in the context of first-century Palestine that their revolutionary character is largely lost on contemporary children. When, for example, children of seven or eight read the story of the Pharisees, who were horrified because Jesus hadn't washed his hands before eating, they understand it in terms of their parents' insistence that they always wash up before meals. But there is a world of difference between ritual washing and washing up for lunch, a difference not obvious to young children.

What about Jesus' impatience with the temple priests and their emphasis on animal sacrifice? Children will agree instinctively with Jesus that doing justly is more pleasing to God than providing an unblemished dove or lamb for temple sacrifice. This attitude is not due to any great spiritual insight, but simply to the fact that a God who would *want* an animal killed to please Him is almost unthinkable to modern children.

And what about the Golden Rule, so popular a subject for Sunday-school lessons? Actually this too is very easily misunderstood by children. One eight-year-old interpreted it to mean that, if someone pinches you, you should pinch him back, because he has done to you what he wants you to do to him. Simply the way it is phrased makes it difficult for children to grasp. The phrasing that occurs in the teachings of Confucius is clearer to a child: "What you do not want done to yourself, do not do to others."

Even when the meaning is clear, we question whether knowledge of a rule has very much impact on children's behavior. A vivid story that embodies an idea makes much more of an impression than a rule; to affect feelings, feelings must be stirred. Jesus was well aware of this, and most of his teaching was in story form. For this reason children are much quicker to respond to the idea of the Golden Rule as embodied in the African story, "The Two Cheats," than in "The Very Short Rule," which is a retelling of Jesus' giving the Golden Rule.[14] But even when children hear the rule in vivid story form, we wonder if it will affect their own living unless certain conditions in their real-life situations make it possible for them to try it. We need to do further research to find out to what degree children are helped to greater maturity even by stories that stir feelings.

As for the historic events that must be retold to explain high points in Jesus' life, they are not easily digested by children either. Yet children in our culture need some knowledge of these events.

"I don't see why, if Jesus was so good, he got killed," said six-year-old Nancy on Good Friday. "I should think everyone would have liked him."

"There seem to have been several reasons," said her father, launching eagerly into the discussion. He had studied theology; it was going to be fun explaining this. "It tells in the gospels —"

"What are the gospels, Daddy?"

"They are the four books in the Bible —"

"I thought the Bible was one book, Daddy."

"The Bible is a collection of books. But wait a minute, let's get back to why Jesus was killed. There seem to have been two main reasons. We think that some of the Jewish people" (*What are the Jewish people, Daddy?*) "thought he was the Messiah" (*What is the Messiah, Daddy?*), "but the Romans" (*Who are the Romans, Daddy?*), "who ruled" (*What's ruled, Daddy?*) "his country didn't want the Jews to have a king." (*Why, Daddy?*)

"Secondly, Jesus believed that animal sacrifice" (*What's that, Daddy?*) "and strict keeping of the law" (*What's that, Daddy?*) "were less important than purity of heart." (*Than what, Daddy?*) "It made the priests very cross." (*Who are they, Daddy?*) And so on.

Perhaps Nancy's father would have been better off to have said simply that Jesus was killed because he preached things people did not want to hear and that not everyone thought Jesus was good. He might have suggested that other great men have been killed, too. A brief retelling of the death of Socrates would be appropriate in such a situation.

There is no more humbling experience than attempting to explain a complicated problem or fact to a child. Interpreting the events in the life of Jesus to a child can afford adults many such humbling moments.

Children of religious liberals also need some understanding of the way the person of Jesus has been treated as a symbol all through the history of the Christian Church. Jesus, who was a real man, living at a specific time, has been seen as a timeless embodiment of many different values. This has been true of other historical figures also.

The symbolic Jesus has appeared in a variety of forms down through Christian history. Actually, this process of turning the historic Jesus of first-century Palestine into a symbolic figure began among his own contemporaries. For those who hoped he was the Messiah, he became the Messiah, the Christ; and so it has been ever since as people have read about Jesus. In the New Testament records themselves, we see evidence of facts altered and characteristics bestowed on Jesus, so that he could be seen as the embodiment of certain values that had special appeal to either a Greek audience, or a Jewish audience, or a combination of these. The Jesus of the fourth gospel or the Jesus in the Epistle to the Hebrews — these are forerunners of the wide variety of symbolic representations of Jesus that are possible.

The Jesus that has affected Western civilization so dramatically has been a series of figures created by the religious fervor or creative intellect of St. Paul, St. Augustine, St. Thomas, Luther, Hegel, Moody, Rauschenbusch, or the contemporary Paul Tillich. Every passionate mystic, every zealous founder of a new denomination or sect, every writer of a fictional life of Jesus has, to a greater or less degree, taken the Jesus that he found in the gospels, or in his private meditation, and fashioned him into a symbolic figure who has stirred and won people. The trouble is that the claim is invariably made that each of these is *the* historic Jesus.

Jesus has been pictured, in almost contradictory ways, as

the Great High Priest, the Prophet, the Logos, the Savior, the Suffering Servant. A study of these symbolic characterizations of Jesus should be a part of the religious education of young people. We believe that our method of introducing comparative myths and legends to children is a sound way to lead up to such a study.

Probably we should have a course for adolescents or older young people in which these symbolic ideas — such as priest, prophet, logos, savior, and so forth — can be studied in a variety of religious traditions, as well as in the Jewish-Christian tradition. Unless we can make a place for the appreciation of symbolic representations of great religious figures, as well as study of the history behind them, our children will be unable to understand or appreciate the art or theology of any of the world's religions.

As liberal religious parents and teachers, we must keep clear our goals as regards the person of Jesus. We want to interpret the questions and comments our children bring in such a way as to clear up confusion, alleviate worry, and enlighten ignorance. But above all we want to protect the real, historic figure from over-simplification, and over-familiarity in the early years of childhood. We also want to guard against the literal interpretation of the various symbolic treatments of Jesus that our children will find in the culture. In so far as we succeed, it may mean that at an appropriate age our children will be eager to undertake a real study of Jesus and to evaluate him for themselves.

12

Children and the Bible

"It's a book all about God."

What do we believe that the Bible actually is? Most religious liberals believe that the Bible is a library of books that contains some of the most important and most treasured early writings of the Jewish people. It contains, also, the earliest books that we have about Jesus and the founding of the Christian Church. It is a book that has shaped Western thought, and that permeates Western ethics and art.

If we believe this, the next logical question to ask is: Which parts of this material are interesting and enriching to children under ten, to older children, and to adults? How can this material best be transmitted to them? Because we believe that for younger children here-and-now experiences are the source of rich religious values, and that for older children religious insight is to be gained from a variety of sources, it will not be of crucial importance whether there is much or little in the Bible that can be used before adulthood.

If these were our only concerns, all would be well. But, as in the other areas we have discussed, years before our children reach an age at which Bible study seems to us advisable they begin to hear about the Bible through various avenues of communication in our culture. And they often hear about it, not in the way that we would like them to, but as a kind of magic holy book.

Its very look sets it apart from other books. It is often very large, with an unusual binding and arrangement of its printed pages. It may be mentioned in a special tone of voice. It must be handled with special care. Sometimes it is an object that resides between two candles on a worship center in Sunday school or on the pulpit in church.

Our children may hear about the Bible as something that is offered as a prize or reward.

"Mother," asked Helen, "may I go to Bible school with Gloria?"

"No," said Helen's mother. "I'd rather you wouldn't."

"Gloria keeps asking me to go. I hate to tell her all the time that I can't go. If I go, and if she can get two other girls to go, she can win a Bible."

"I'll call up her mother," said Helen's mother. "I'll explain why I'd rather not have you go. Will that help?"

"Yes," said Helen. "I don't see why she wants to win a Bible anyhow. She's already won two Bibles."

In many public schools the Bible is read daily without a word of explanation, and felt, nonetheless, to have deep spiritual value. Somehow, because the Bible has been read and the flag saluted, the day is supposed to be automatically off to a propitious start.

In all of these instances the Bible is being treated as a symbol. It is precisely what our culture does in the area of patriotism — teaching children to wave flags before they can have any appreciation of the political and social realities that make a flag something to be proud of. The result may be a society of flag-wavers whose actions and real convictions deny the realities the flag is supposed to symbolize. Treating the Bible primarily as a symbol may produce men who build monuments to honor the prophets whom their fathers slew. We do not want our children to be Bible-wavers, with no knowledge of its real meanings.

We prefer to encourage our children to develop an attitude toward the Bible based on their knowledge of what the

Bible is, rather than on how others feel about the Bible. When the Bible was the chief — and in some cases the only — printed material in the home, treating the Bible as a symbol was less likely to have the unhappy effect that it now has. But today, in a world flooded with other reading matter more easily understood than the Bible, an increasing number of people feel a reverence for the Bible who at the same time are abysmally ignorant of what is in it.

This may be another factor contributing to the crowded state of our Sunday schools. Many parents are searching for someone to teach their children what lies between these covers that they were taught to revere but now rarely read. All too often these adults believe that all true religion is contained within this Holy Book. Although many adults seem to be able to do without the Bible themselves, except for what the minister reads to them on Sunday, they would like their children to "know the Bible." The irony is that there are fewer and fewer people equipped to teach the Bible as more people clamor to have it taught to their children. The Bible is often thought of as one thinks of good manners — the sooner children "have" it, the better.

Those who first build up a picture of the Bible through the attitude of others toward it, and before they themselves can properly understand what it actually is all about, will have to tear down the false picture before a truer one can take its place. This is too painful a process for a good many adults; they may either cling to the false picture for the rest of their lives or never bother to try to arrive at a fresh understanding of the Bible. This is precisely the kind of experience that we are eager to avoid in the religious education of our children — although to avoid it is not easy in our culture.

Why have so many Christians believed that the Bible should be taught to children as young as possible? The primary theological reason has been the belief that God speaks in the Bible and reveals Himself there as He has never revealed Himself elsewhere; if children are to know God, they must know the Bible. In the past, and with fundamentalist Christians still, there has not been much concern as to how much of the Bible was understandable to children. Just to be exposed to it was felt to have value.

This is not the case now, at least among the intellectual orthodox, and the situation poses all kinds of problems for them. James D. Smart, who was the editor-in-chief of the elaborate Presbyterian Faith and Life Curriculum, writes: "Nothing in the Bible was written specifically for children. From beginning to end it is an adult book. . . ." He then goes on to say: "When we use the Bible with children, *as we must do,* we should begin by recognizing that we are adapting to the situation of children material that was written for adults, and that the important thing is to retain the original meaning, but to interpret it in terms comprehensible to children."[1]

This sounds very much like wanting to have your cake and eat it, too. If something really is adult material, how can it be so interpreted as to become children's material and yet retain *its original meaning?* To say that it is adult material means that a person must have reached a certain maturity through his own experience before he can understand it; and such a process cannot be speeded up. Yet many people feel that, to make God known to their children, the Bible must be used. They must then not only try to find material that can be used with children in the light of what educators tell us children of various ages can understand, but also decide how children are supposed to interpret the Biblical material they are given. For the intellectual orthodox do not want their children to believe literally all they read.

How, then, are the children supposed to interpret the Bible? Dr. Smart quotes and comments on the following incident. "One nine-year-old, on the way home from school, was heard to say to a companion: 'I guess what's in the Bible isn't really true. I am going to stick with the scientists.'" Dr. Smart comments: "Not to give that child an understanding that Genesis, chapters one to three, is not authoritative history or geography or astronomy or biology, but is authoritative revelation of who God is and who we are, and how our world and humanity are related to God, is nothing less than criminal neglect."[2]

What would it mean for a child of nine to grasp that the creation stories in Genesis are "an authoritative revelation of who God is"? Probably Dr. Smart means that the Jewish myths "reveal" God as Creator and man as creature. So have many of the creation myths of other cultures. But the intellectual orthodox cannot allow the Jewish myths to be put on a level with non-Biblical myths. The Bible myths must be uniquely revelatory of "who God is" and how man is related to God.

Actually, all of these myths *were* the geography, astronomy, biology of early pre-scientific peoples, though they cannot be ours. We who live in a scientific era owe earlier generations a debt of gratitude for having wondered and thought and tried to make sense of the world in which they found themselves.

We are confident that children between six and ten can be helped to see that the old creation myths and other myths of the Jews show some real insight, as do the early myths of other peoples. As suggested earlier, we would always present myths from a variety of cultures, for a comparative presentation demonstrates to children the universality of the phenomena with which these early thinkers wrestled. A comparative presentation also protects children, still prone to literal-mindedness, from the worry of "Did it *really* happen?"

In an earlier chapter we mentioned a little girl who was very upset by the Noah story. If she had been told this story in a comparative arrangement, we doubt that she would have taken it so literally and been so frightened by it. Of course, an orthodox teacher who believes it literally or wants it believed literally cannot treat it in this way. We know, however, that flood myths or legends are a part of the story heritage of many cultures. In fact, the whole planet seems to have emerged from a very watery beginning. It is also true that many early cultures grew up near great rivers which frequently flooded what seemed to be "the whole earth." The flood story in our Bible goes back to Sumerian lore, the fruit of a culture situated between the Tigris and the Euphrates. The hero in this version is the culture hero, Gilgamesh. There is need for a book of myths for children between six and twelve that would contain, among other things, flood myths from many cultures. Perhaps also it might present several myths that attempt to account for the variety of human languages, as does the Biblical story of the Tower of Babel.

It is a good practice to give some historic or cultural background when presenting these myths and legends, indicating what the people were trying to understand or express and the setting in which their thinking occurred. With such handling, we believe that myths and legends can enrich a child's developing religious ideas. The tragedy of the orthodox way of presenting the Bible myths and legends as literal truth, or as *the true* myth, is that it forces children to make such narrow choices: Did it really happen? Is it really the *best* myth? We believe that no such narrow choices need be made in relation to this kind of material.

During the writing of this chapter the following conversation took place with a thirteen-year-old boy. He was working for his "God and Country" Boy Scout award. He had attended an orthodox church school since the age of five.

"What would you say the Bible is?" we asked.

"It's all about Jesus," he replied.

"All of it?" we asked.

"No," he said, reconsidering. "The New Testament has about God making the earth, and it has about Noah. I was just reading about him for my Boy Scout award. God found favor in Noah's sight."

"That was the *Old* Testament," we said. "And wasn't the favor finding the other way around? But what about that flood? What do you think is the point of that story?"

"Well, I guess so we'd know what happened. But, gee, I don't see how they can remember way back then."

We let the conversation drop, sadly, thinking how much poorer in spirit this boy was than children with whom these old stories had been enjoyed for what they are — not accurate history nor authoritative revelation, but the early thoughts and stories of an ancient people. Our children need to inherit these tales as they need to inherit the tales from other Bibles. We believe that our new way of approaching these materials will insure their inheritance; it will keep these myths from being cast aside because they cannot be believed, or being believed literally, thereby cutting the believer off from the thought world of today.

For the children of orthodoxy, the first contact with comparative religion in college or elsewhere is very often so upsetting that the entire structure of their faith may be toppled. For children who have been guided in these new ways, comparative religion is part and parcel of the structure of their faith, and every contact with other religious traditions strengthens its foundations.

We do, however, have problems to cope with in regard to the Bible. Our need is not to figure out ways of teaching the Bible before our children can grasp the material in it. Rather we must give children all the help we can to interpret what they hear about it and, in so far as possible, to prevent a false picture from being built up about the Bible before they are ready to study it. Although this may sound negative, we believe it can be done in a way that is essentially positive.

For one thing, when the occasion presents itself, we will need to state clearly the few facts about the make-up of the Bible that are comprehensible to children under ten. The Bible is not one book, but a collection of sixty-six books written down by men who lived in one small area of the world. Parts of it are much older than other parts. The books are of many different kinds.

We have started with children as young as six to hammer away at simple facts like these; but we must confess that it is astonishing how few of them are retained. Sometimes we think that it might help if all the books of the Bible were bound separately in covers that gave a clue to the kinds of material in them, with bold pictures, large type, and inviting format. It might keep children from developing the false picture of one book — and a not very interesting-looking one at that.

Whenever any material from the Bible is brought up, let us explore with children, in as much detail as their age level allows, the kind of writing that it represents. Is it a poem, a legend, a myth, a sermon, a biography, a love song, a play, a letter, history, laws a wise saying or just what?

There are several reasons we would try to do this with children. On the one hand it encourages an attitude of finding out about this one-book library and helps children make a start at breaking it down into its component parts. Children very early get the impression that if something is from the Bible, they need only to look reverent and stop thinking. This we want to avoid. Also, it might help children to see the inappropriateness of always approaching Biblical material with such questions as "Is it true?" "Can I believe it?" Children must learn to bring a variety of questions to Biblical material. Isn't half the job of becoming educated learning to ask the right questions?

Of the history in the Bible we must ask: "Did this really happen, or has the record been tampered with?" Of the poetry: "Is it rich, enlightening, refreshing to one's feelings?" Of the legends: "Why were these stories imagined? What facts lie back of them?" Of the myths: "What truths do they contain? Do we know other myths like them?"

For sound educational reasons, the process of explaining the actual make-up of the Bible to children cannot advance very far before children reach the age of ten. We do not think it is worth while, therefore, to develop church-school courses in the Bible for these younger children. The little that can be done, we think, is better accomplished informally at home or as discussion comes up in a church-school class. Our success will depend to a large degree on our own knowledge of the make-up and content of the Bible. Actually it is we adults who need the courses on the Bible more than the children. Where is the liberal student of the Bible who will write a scholastically sound, honest, one-volume Bible commentary for liberal religious adults?

We may also wish to begin to establish with children an understanding of the sequence of historical events in the Bible. Here too we will not expect very great results much before the age of ten. As far as possible, however, we want to encourage an awareness of how ideas of God and ideas of right and wrong have changed — and how they change even inside the covers of the Bible. One of the unhappy by-products of orthodox approaches to the Bible is that they increase the likelihood that children will think of all the characters in the Bible as contemporary with one another. An approach that encourages a reading of the Old Testament in the light of the New; that puts on an equal level God's actions in the Noah legend, and His actions in the life of

Jesus; that urges children to ask of any Biblical passage, "What is God saying to me, through this?" — this has many unfortunate results. It blurs, distorts, and conceals the actual content of the Bible and reduces or exalts to one level of importance all the meanings to be found in it.

An eleven-year-old, who had an unusually high I.Q., was asked what he thought the Bible was about. "In the Bible," he said, "Jesus tells us how the world began."

"Jesus wasn't there," said his seven-year-old friend. "The world was made millions and millions of years ago. There weren't any people around. Do you mean you *believe* the Bible story about how the world was made?"

"Yes," said the eleven-year-old, in a doubtful but reverent voice. "Jesus must have known all about His Father and how He made the world."

The orthodox church-school teachers who had instructed this boy might have been disappointed at what he had made of the factual parts of the lessons they had taught him, although they would perhaps have been pleased with his attitude of reverence.

This brings us to a second positive step we must take. Our children need help in understanding why the majority in our culture believe the Bible to be a supernatural book. At the age of seven or eight, most Sunday-school children, if asked what the Bible is, will reply, "It's a book all about God," or "It's God's book."

"Tommy said that the Bible is God's book and that if you drop it on the floor, you might die," said six-year-old Henry. "His grandmother told him that."

"That's Tommy's grandmother's way of saying the Bible is a special book," said Henry's mother. "Part of the Bible is old stories that people have loved. All peoples in the world have had such stories, trying to explain things like why the world is here, or telling about great heroes. Some of these stories are so old that we think they were told even before people knew how to write. Because people could not write, the wisdom of earlier generations could only be preserved and handed on to the next generation by word of mouth. Very often only very special persons were allowed to tell these stories and sometimes it was believed that the gods and spirits had told them to the earliest ancestors of men.

"It was important that the stories be handed on as unchanged as possible. But because they were not written at first and were told in many separate places, many different versions of some of them actually grew up. When men learned to write, it was easier to make sure that not a dot or comma in a story was changed lest some of the ancient wisdom should be lost. Often several different versions of the stories were known, and those that wrote them down sometimes tried to combine them into one. We can see that this has been done in many places in our Bible.[3] So you see, books with such old stories in them *are* special, although you wouldn't really die if you dropped one of them on the floor."

To account for the existence of sacred scriptures in some such way as has been suggested here, we have found both interesting and convincing to children. They seem to understand readily the emotional need that is met by the insistence that not a word of a beloved story be changed. They also seem to feel that, if something is written down, it is special and ought to be read *as is*. And when children hear two versions of a story, they think that only one can be the *true* one, or the *real* one.

It is a good idea to introduce early the fact that our Bible is only one Bible, and that there are many other sacred books or Bibles.

Two seven-year-old boys were talking at lunch. Terry was from an orthodox home.

"Well, you can say the Lord's Prayer all you want," said

Terry. Then, half joking, he went on, "But you and I will never see God. When we die, we'll go down to the 'hot place,' not up to Heaven."

"Why are you so sure there is a Heaven?" challenged his friend Bruce. "How do you know you would see God if you did go to Heaven? Let's see you prove there is a Heaven anyway."

"Well, the Bible says there is one, so I guess that's proof all right," said Terry with finality.

"Oh well," retorted Bruce, "if you want to use the Bible for proof, that's up to you."

Bruce's mother made a further suggestion. "You know, Terry, there are many people in the world who don't even know our Bible. They have other books which they use for proof of their beliefs. But I wonder if you can prove a question like whether there's a Heaven by looking in a book — our Bible or anyone else's."

This was a good suggestion. The mother's observation about other Bibles is the kind that helps to correct the misconception that the Bible is "unique," "mysterious," "not to be examined closely." This must be done if the Bible is going to be free to function in children's lives as something more than a symbol or a magic revelation of truth.

Another important attitude toward the Bible that often calls for an explanation from us is one touched on several times already in this book — the Bible considered predominantly as the Story of Salvation. The fact is that, for a large proportion of those who still read their Bible, it is not a collection of books but really one connected Story, the Greatest Story Ever Told, the story of God's salvation of man from sin and error. This attitude turns the Bible into one great myth.

The Old Story begins with the creation of the world and the first man and woman. It tells of their fall, through Satan,

and then, age after age, of God's attempts to win man back
to Himself. It tells of the mighty heroes, Noah, Abraham,
Moses, David, and others to whom He gave miraculous
powers, but all to no avail. Men still chose evil. Finally the
Old Story tells how God decided to bring man back to Himself by sacrificing his dearest possession, His only Son. The
drama culminates with the promise of salvation to all who
accept Christ as their Savior; the promise of Hell for those
who do not accept Him; and the promise of His coming
again in glory.

This, many people say, is the story that runs through the
Bible. This is really what the Bible is all about. Not only
is this an attitude held by fundamentalist Christians, but it
is an increasingly popular point of view among intellectual
Christians. The reason for the popularity of this point of
view is understandable, and its appeal to scholarly Christians
is well accounted for in a statement by Dr. Smart.

He tells of the upsetting experience he had when he returned to the pulpit after nine years of advanced study on
the Old Testament. He found himself so aware of the problems of Biblical criticism that he had no message to preach
from the Old Testament that was of interest to a Christian
congregation. So he "had to start at the beginning again, to
read the Old Testament as the record of a revelation of God
and, moreover, as the record of a revelation that had its
center and climax in Jesus Christ."[4] In other words, he now
chose to read the Bible as the Story of Salvation.

If one looks at the Bible in this way, it is truly "a book
all about God." It is important to distinguish this symbolic
way of thinking about the Bible from an historic approach
to the Bible, which sees it as a collection of books of a variety
of kinds, containing different religious ideas. We would like
our children to read this old story as it has been gathered up
out of the Bible and retold in *The Old Story of Salvation* by
Sophia L. Fahs. They can read it appreciatively by about

the age of twelve. But because younger children hear talk
that can only be understood if one thinks of the Bible as
this salvation story, children need to know the large outline
of the story even before they are twelve.

In the first chapter of this book, we mentioned a little girl
who was worried that Jesus would take her up in his arms.
She might have been told that this idea was part of the way
some people understand the Bible. It is an old way of understanding about Jesus. It isn't what we think really happened or is going to happen — but a kind of "picture way"
of thinking. She will study it when she is older.

Some children, who have taken literally the unpleasant
possibility of "being washed in the blood of the lamb" or
have heard of "The Most Precious Blood of Jesus," may also
be helped by relating these remarks to the Old Story of
Salvation. Unfortunately, before seven or eight children
can make very little sense out of the idea of animal sacrifice,
and they do not easily see a similarity between Jesus' death
and the slaughter of a lamb. But if the child is worried about
it, we should make a stab at explaining it.

It would seem best, then, for parents and teachers to
familiarize themselves with this story. Mrs. Fahs's retelling
of the story, together with her relevant questions about it,
is an ideal place for parents and teachers to do this. In this
book the material has been organized as one great drama,
according to a plan that St. Augustine used in the fifth century. In the first section of the book, using Biblical language, the author presents the story without comment. In
the second section she raises a series of questions that will
undoubtedly occur to the thoughtful reader. She presents
pertinent data, historic, scientific, theological, that will aid
readers in their study and evaluation of the story. The third
section of the book describes briefly ways in which this story
has been depicted in the arts. In conclusion Mrs. Fahs pre-

sents seven different answers to the question: What, then, shall we do with this old story?

Of course, the process of turning parts of the Bible into one continuous story was begun long before the Christian era. Students of the Old Testament have given names and dates to the different "editors" who took old myths, sagas, legends, and actual history and wove them together, rewrote them, and doctored them to prove various theories of history. The untangling of the work of these editors has been the concern of Biblical scholars and critics for over one hundred years. Their work has disclosed the historic Bible to us. We want our young people and adults to know this historic Bible. We believe that such knowledge can make the reading of the Bible an exciting enterprise. Unlike Dr. Smart, we think it could be presented to Christian congregations and made fascinating and religiously enriching to them. It does not seem to us intellectually honest or necessary to read just one great message into the Bible in order to keep congregations interested.

Finally, there will be occasions when liberal religious parents find that they need to tell their young children actual incidents from the Bible or stories about the "heroes of Israel" in order to explain certain cultural phenomenon. One mother, a religious liberal, said: "I agree that these old Bible stories aren't the main part of my children's religious education. And I know, too, how disillusioned I was after attending a traditional Sunday school for fourteen years to discover in a Bible course at college that David wasn't such a wonderful character really, and that much of the Bible wasn't literally true, as I had been led to think. Still I want my children to know these stories. They are a part of our culture. Can't I just read to them at bedtime from a Bible story book?"

Unfortunately, there is no such thing as "just reading" a

story. When children are told a story they take it into themselves and make of it what their own hopes and fears, understanding and needs, compel them to. In all the Bible story
books we have seen, theological and ethical concepts that
we do not wish to hand on uncritically to our children are
taken for granted. Do we believe that God especially chooses
people, and that some of these people are as self-centered as
Joseph, or cheat like Jacob, or rob another man of his wife
as David did? We value our children's developing religious
consciousness too highly to "just read" these stories, without
helping them to understand the ways of thinking embedded
in the stories. Perhaps someone will be able to arrange some
of these old tales in a comparative setting and present sagas
and legends from several early cultures.

The "New Beacon Series in Religious Education" contains
a good deal of Biblical material, but predominantly for children over ten. The books are based on the findings of Biblical
scholars in the various areas. The story of Joseph, for instance, has been vividly retold for children between seven
and nine, with almost no theological content.[5] It is presented
as a saga that was handed down over the years: the story
of a family crisis and its felicitous denouement that affected
a whole people. The advantage of the way it has been told
is that modern children can know a good story without
becoming involved in the theology that permeates the Bible
version. In any case it is likely that the original story of
Joseph was put in its Biblical theological setting by a late
editor.

The legend of Moses has been treated quite differently; it
has been retold for ten- and eleven-year-olds.[6] The account
from the Bible is given at the end of each chapter. The
chapters themselves are an attempt to find what history there
may be back of the legend. One may question whether the
miracles in the story should be rationalized as they are here

— or whether they should be treated as tall tales, written to enhance the figure of Moses. Very often children will be familiar with Negro spirituals that can only be understood when the Moses story is known; references to the Ten Commandments, the burning bush, the plagues, the dividing of the waters, are frequent in our culture. Parents may therefore wish to retell this story for children between six and ten, keeping in mind the thought that it is material children should grow into — not outgrow.

There are also several stories from the Bible in *From Long Ago and Many Lands,* for seven- to nine-year-olds.[7] But for the Biblical period from the death of Moses to the dividing of the kingdom, *The Drama of Ancient Israel* will be the best source to use.[8] This has been prepared for children twelve and older. Here the stories of Joshua and the walls of Jericho, of Gideon, of Samson, of David, of Solomon, and others are retold. The author gives the historic setting that some scholars believe lies behind these stories, and he attempts to disentangle history from legend. Parents and teachers should familiarize themselves with this book and be ready to tell the tales as the children need them, giving some of the history and culture that make them understandable old stories, not miraculous events that call for blind acceptance or rejection.

Moses is not the only figure in history to have been found in a basket in the bulrushes; nor is David the only hero to have killed lions and beasts as a small boy, and giants as a man. Parents might well acquaint themselves with the Sumerian Sargon,[9] who earlier than Moses was put in a basket as a baby and became a great lawgiver. Parents need to help children see that David of Jerusalem and our Davy Crockett have been treated in similar fashion. If a parent knows the facts of comparative mythology and legend-making, plus the actual history and culture that provide the stuff out of which the color and warmth of the legend comes, he can feel that he is opening doors of understanding to children, rather than asking them to believe the incredible.

We still have much to find out about the best ways to make the Bible a vital part of our children's inheritance. With children under ten, our main concern will be to give them a few facts about the make-up and content of the Bible as circumstances demand, and to help them begin to understand why the majority in our culture believe as they do about the Bible, treating it as a holy symbol. At the same time we want to be laying a foundation for a real study of Biblical material as soon as they are ready for it.

In this way we hope to keep the Bible an open library of books, which stand as a challenge to our children's curiosity and intellect when they are ready to grapple with it. We do not want our children bored at the mention of the Bible, or ready with a neat label for what it is all about before they have ever really looked inside its covers. Thus we may legitimately hope that someday they will have an accurate knowledge of the Bible, as well as a deep appreciation for certain parts of it.

13

The Cycle of Life and Death

"I don't ever want to die."

A young father found himself deep in a discussion with his four-year-old daughter. Martha had lost a little friend in an automobile accident. She asked many questions about the event. It upset her that Elaine was to be put in the ground. Wouldn't Elaine mind having the dirt in her face? Wouldn't she get wet when it rained? Wouldn't she be lonesome?

The young father did not know just how to explain to his daughter what happens at death. After a few rather vague remarks, he decided, in order to bring the conversation to a close, to tell Martha that her friend had gone to Heaven, a place where all people go when they die. To his confusion, he found that this answer, instead of satisfying his daughter, opened the door to a flood of even less answerable questions. Could Elaine take her tricycle to Heaven? What do people eat there? Why couldn't she go up there and see Elaine?

In the end the father realized that by introducing the traditional idea of Heaven he had created far more problems than he had solved. As a result of being given this idea, the child was now asking questions about the concept of Heaven, instead of asking questions about what she herself had experienced: the fact that people die.

The actual experience of losing something or someone by death is almost inescapably a part of the lives of most children as young as four. It may be a grandparent who dies, or a beloved pet, or some creature found in the yard.

175

Even a dead fly, swatted in the kitchen, poses the question: What happens when something dies?

Rare indeed is the child who by five or six has not either been consciously taught, or has not picked up from others, an answer that goes something like this: When a person dies his soul or spirit, the part of a person that you cannot see, goes to Heaven, and his body is put in the ground. Adults are not so sure just what happens when animals die, even though pets may be as sorely missed as people who have died. Also, by the age of six or seven, even those children who have not been purposely indoctrinated about Hell have heard of it and are fascinated. Heaven, Hell, angels, and the Devil are common topics of conversation among children of primary age.

These concepts excite comment and discussion both because the fact of death is so arresting, and because these traditional ways of interpreting what happens after death are so interestingly specific. They are also very confusing, and to some children worrisome. As with the idea of God, many people have thought that, regardless of what they as adults believe, children need a specific and concrete answer because that is how children think. We agree that children think concretely, but we question whether the concrete answers of traditional religion are the kind of answers that actually satisfy children. We also question whether these make the experience of death more understandable to children and whether they foster in children healthy attitudes toward life.

One mother describes this incident. Her three-year-old son had been very close to his grandfather. When the grandfather died, the boy was told that grandfather had gone to Heaven, a place up in the sky.

One day, after a rainstorm, the mother was sweeping the porch. Her son was playing in the yard with the grandfather's old hat, which had been given to him. The mother heard him talking to someone.

"I'm sorry, grandpa," said the little boy, looking up at the sky. "I'm sorry I left your hat out in the rain. I won't do it again."

The mother reports: "At first, I thought, 'Isn't that sweet. He's just as close to him as ever.' But the more I thought about it, and the more times I overheard these conversations, the more I began to worry and wonder whether what we had told him was good for him. Didn't he need to accept the fact that grandpa was really gone, rather than to be given the idea that somehow life goes on?"

We agree with this mother that what the young child seems to need in his first experiences with death is to grasp what has really happened. Someone or something was alive and now is not alive. How can this be? What does it mean to be alive? Differentiating between what is alive and not alive is a long, slow process that goes on for years. The child of eighteen months heedlessly steps on an ant in the dirt as readily as a pebble; he is aware of no difference. The two-year-old, squatting, watches the caterpillar walk along the sidewalk; if he squashes it, he realizes, without really understanding, that he has done something to it. The three- or four-year-old may be able to verbalize the difference between the living and the lifeless, realizing that his toy kitty and his pet kitty are very different kinds of beings. But because children can verbalize the difference this does not mean they actually feel the wonder of it. There is a tremendous mystery summed up in the word "alive."

This was made vivid to a six-year-old boy. One evening, soon after a new baby brother had come home from the hospital, the thermometer read sixteen below zero. The big brother and his mother went into the baby's room to see if the baby was covered and warm.

"Put your hand inside his sleeper," said the mother.

"Isn't he warm!" said the little boy.

"Now feel the metal on the end of his bed."

"It's freezing!" said the six-year-old.

"Just think!" said the mother. "He's such a tiny little baby and yet he can keep himself warm! The bed has to get just as cold as the air in the room, but the baby makes his own warmth. He's alive. I can see why some speak about the 'spark of life.'"

Although we do not know what aliveness is, we can heighten our own and our children's sensitivity to its amazing quality. We can hand life on through our own bodies; we can snuff it out in a variety of ways. But we cannot make it new, out of nothing. Life is something that commands our respect, even our reverence. It is, in the most profound sense, a gift. Rather than *tell* this to young children, we want them to experience it. This is one of the main concerns in our new ways in religious education: to share with little children first-hand experiences of a living Universe. Only when they appreciate the mystery of life can they appreciate the mystery of death.

In the "Martin and Judy" books, one of the basic emphases is to sharpen children's awareness of the differences between what is alive and what is not alive. Judy, for example, sees how different her doll and her baby sister are: one forever the same weight, height, and inertness, the other growing, learning, and alive.[1] In "The Bird That Could Not Fly" Martin and Judy are impressed by the amazing fact that it does no good to prop the dead bird up and try to make it walk, for life has somehow gone out of it. It is dead.[2]

It seems to us that little children need to realize this unmistakably. They need this more than they need to have us rush ahead and assure them that in some sense the bird, or pet, or friend, or grandparent is not *really* dead. When the goldfish floats on the top of the water, or the cat lies motionless in the road, it is dead — and no words can change this fact. Something basic and irrevocable has happened. We need not dwell long over this reality, but we should not blur or hide it.

A second basic emphasis we want to make in children's experiences with death is that death is a necessary part of life. In order to do this we can bring to children's attention the fact that all life passes through a cycle. Everything, including human beings, is born, grows, buds, flowers, forms seed, withers, and dies. All plants and animals — though some in very rudimentary fashion — exhibit this pattern.

The youngest children will experience each phase of the cycle as a separate phenomenon: buds, new leaves, fruit, fallen leaves; babies, children, grownups, old people. Only gradually do children begin to realize that all the steps in the cycle are linked together. The flower on the apple tree will finally be seen as the forerunner of the bright red fruit, and the number of blossoms on the horse chestnut tree will gradually be discovered to be a good indication of the number of precious velvet-smooth horse chestnuts that will be gathered in the fall.

Children should also have their attention drawn to the interaction between various forms of life that bring about the completion of the cycle of life. Not only is the work of the bee essential for the pollination of some flowers, but the lowly fungus on the rotting trees does a necessary work in breaking down materials in the dead tree and returning them to the soil, so that other living things can make use of them again.

> The soil feeds the tree
> And the tree drops its leaves,
> And the leaves make soil
> And the soil feeds the tree —

Over and over again.
It never begins and it never ends,
Nothing is old, and nothing is new
And nothing is ever lost.[3]

Books such as *Animal Babies, The Family Finds Out, A Brand New Baby,* and *How Miracles Abound* suggest some of the kinds of experiences we need to share with children to sharpen their sensitivity, both to the amazing quality of aliveness in things, and to the cyclic character of the life process.[4]

The story "The Mustard Seed Medicine" from Buddhist scriptures is a gem.[5] It expresses the idea that death is inevitably a part of life; that life and death are woven from one fabric, and that we must accept the one with the other. To hear such a story can give children, seven and older, the first legitimate certainty we can have on the subject of death — the certainty that it will come to all of us, and that it is the essence of wisdom to accept this.

It is interesting to compare this story with the one from the Christian scriptures that credits Jesus with the ability to raise the dead. In one story, a teacher is revered because he raised the dead and put death off; in the other the teacher is honored because he helped a woman to accept death as an essential phase in the cycle of life. Which attitude do we wish to encourage: one that hopes to put off death or one that accepts it as a part of life?

Another story that stimulates children's thinking is the myth "The Road to Olelpanti," from the collection *Beginnings of Life and Death.*[6] In this story early men struggle with the question of whether it would be better to have old people capable of becoming young again, or to accept the pattern of new life appearing and the old dying. Other myths in this collection can help children evaluate some of the other old answers to the question: Why do men die?

The even more basic rhythms of the Universe itself stand as a mighty backdrop to the cycles of life on our earth. We follow the round of the seasons, spring, summer, fall, and winter; the rising and setting of the sun; the waxing and waning of the moon; the steady flow of the tides in and out; the wheeling of the stars and planets overhead.

Are we seeking to bring an awareness of these rhythms into the consciousness of our children and to have this awareness function as a source of spiritual refreshment? We adults realize that in all cultures, the world over, the seasons of a person's life and the seasons of the year have been celebrated in the symbolism and poetry of the dominant myths of each culture. We realize that back of baptism, confirmation, weddings, and funeral ceremonials — back of spring, summer, fall, and winter festivals — lie the natural facts of birth, puberty, marriage, and death, and the journey of the earth around the sun, once each year, with all that it involves.

In most cultures the sacramental observances and festivals are made vivid and important to children before they have any awareness of the basic universal realities that such ceremonies are celebrating. Religious liberals wish to proceed in just the opposite direction — first developing children's sensitivities to the basic phenomena that have evoked these universal observances.

When our children come with questions about festivals and sacraments of various groups, let us help them relate specific practices to the deep, universal, natural roots from which they spring. We will not be able to do this significantly if we have not really sought to develop our children's awareness of these basic realities in our positive religious-education programs. We will also want to give children any historical explanations that are relevant and understandable. Religious liberals are aware of a need to experiment in more meaningful services for their own celebrations of these personal holy days and seasonal holidays.

The fact that our bodies, like all other animal and vegetable life, go through a cycle may seem acceptable to many of us. But are we content to say that this is the whole story? This conversation occurred one supper time.

"I don't ever want to die," announced the nine-year-old daughter in the family.

"Why not?" asked her father.

"I just don't," she said.

"I want to live a hundred years," said her seven-year-old brother.

"It's strange to think of things happening and us not being here to know about them," said the daughter.

"Well, they happened before you were born too, dope," said her brother.

"Yes, but you can read about those, dope," said the nine-year-old.

"And you can't read after you're dead," said the father.

"No," said the little girl, as she picked up her spoon. "I always want to be here."

Many of us are quite confused in our thinking on the subject of immortality, lumping together three rather different ideas. There is, for example, the fact that part of our very bodies lives on in our children and our children's children. Our bodies are a link in the chain of life that extends back to the first life on earth and may well go on to the last life on earth. Even the part that goes into the ground may ultimately be taken up and used again by living organisms. This is a very tangible and material kind of immortality that can be readily grasped by children of seven and older. The idea of Heaven is not involved. It is immortality in this world. Children enjoy exploring the implications of this idea.

There is also the immortality of influence. This immortality too involves no concept of Heaven; it is concerned with the effects of our lives that go on and on in this world. For it is a fact that our thoughts and actions live on in those whom our lives touch, and continue to affect the world after we are gone. Whether for good or evil, this influence continues. The mother's loving caress as well as her hasty slap — both continue to ruffle the surface waters and the hidden depths of life, long after they occur. The saints and prophets live on in this way, but so do men of ill will in the unhappy consequences of their acts. This immortality also reaches backward in time, as well as forward, for we are heirs of the ideas, discoveries, and mistakes of all those who have gone before. Human experience is a continuous piece, both for our bodies and for our minds.

It is very interesting to discuss this idea of immortality with children of primary age and older. We may ask, for example, what the labor ballad of Joe Hill means when it says:

> I dreamed I saw Joe Hill last night,
> Alive as you and me.
> Says I, "But Joe you're ten years dead."
> "I never died," says he.
> "I never died," says he.
>
> And standing there as big as life
> And smiling with his eyes,
> Joe says, "What they forgot to kill
> Went on to organize,
> Went on to organize." [7]

If explaining about strikes and organizing seems too stiff a job, the problem can be discussed in relation to a familiar song like John Brown. "John Brown's body lies a mould'ring in the ground . . . but his soul goes marching on." How does it go marching on? What is his soul?

This brings us to the third kind of immortality that we need to think through if we are going to help our children clarify their own thinking and interpret what they hear from others. Was John Brown's soul just his influence? Is this what "soul" really means? Or should this word be saved to stand for something more specific than influence?

With the youngest children we prefer not to objectify the essential qualities of a living person as either a soul or a "wonder part." In our own experience we have not found that children spontaneously think of the living part of a person or pet separately from the body. When we tell children that there is a soul or spirit that does not die and that is not put into the ground, they seem confused. They do not yet have enough experience to feel the problems for which this idea is supposed to be a solution.

We do, however, want to encourage children's thinking about the fact that what we love in a living person is not just the tangible body. In one story in the "Martin and Judy" books, Judy plays a game with her father in which she tries to touch the part of her Daddy that she loves; she finds it is not a single part of the body that can be touched.[8] This, as we suggested in the discussion on God, is a helpful way to encourage children to think about the fact that there is a sense in which things are *real* and yet intangible.

It does not follow, however, that these intangible real qualities can exist apart from a bodily form. The beauty of the flower is real, but the tangible flower has to exist for the beauty to exist. When the flower fades the beauty of the flower passes out of existence, except as it has been seen and appreciated by someone, or as its pollen is spread and it returns to the soil from which it came.

Is it the same with people? When our bodies are gone as individually existing things, is our real, intangible self gone as an individually existing thing too? Many children we know have been content to say that it is.

Is there an entity separate from our bodies, as so many religious groups have believed, a soul or spirit that enters the body at birth and leaves it at death, that goes on — in a place traditionally referred to as Heaven or, as some believe, its counterpart Hell? Or are our thoughts and feelings and beliefs — all the parts that make up our "I" — just something that has reality in relation to our body? When the body dies, does the "I" go out of existence? Is it just our language that makes us think there is an "I" separate from the body? Certainly there is good evidence that as the body deteriorates in sickness or senility the "I" deteriorates too. If there were a soul that entered the body at birth and was shaped and developed during one's life, would it go on after death as we were at our prime, or as we were at death? And what if one died as an infant?

We should be frank and honest when children ask such questions as these. We may say: These are the kind of questions about which no one can speak with certainty; but they are questions that all people have asked. When children see the kinds of problems involved, then it seems to us very valuable to acquaint them with other peoples' solutions to these problems.

The story "Big Questions" by Katherine Wensberg is a fine example of a family doing the kind of mental exploring on the subject of death that we all ought to do, as the occasions arise within our own families.[9] In *Beginnings of Life and Death*, the section entitled, "Our Own Wonderings About Death" is another example of open, frank exploration of the subject. Instead of feeling guilty because we don't *know* what happens after death, we should welcome our children's questions as occasions to explore the problem with them.

The story "A Musician and His Trumpet" tells how one ancient teacher of India answered the question, "What is it that happens when a person dies?"[10] *Their Search for God: Ways of Worship in the Orient* is a fine source book for beliefs of some of the contemporary great religions on the subject of death.[11]

A very moving book that can be read in two or three reading-out-loud sessions with mature primary children and juniors is *The Big Wave* by Pearl Buck. Sharing this book with children actually affords a vicarious experience of losing someone in death. In the story a tidal wave wipes out the whole family of one little boy, leaving him to be brought up by a friend's father and mother. This father and his son Kino are talking over what has happened. The little boy is upset to think that death may strike them so suddenly in Japan, either from tidal wave or earthquake.

"To live in the presence of death makes us brave and strong," Kino's father replied. "That is why our people never fear death. We see it too often and we do not fear it. To die a little later or a little sooner does not matter. But to live bravely, to love life, to see how beautiful the trees are and the mountains, yes, and even the sea, to enjoy work because it produces food for life — in these things we Japanese are a fortunate people. We love life because we live in danger. We do not fear death because we understand that life and death are necessary to each other."

"What is death?" Kino asked.

"Death is the great gateway," Kino's father said. His face was not at all sad. Instead, it was quiet and happy.

"The gateway — where?" Kino asked again.

Kino's father smiled. "Can you remember when you were born?"

Kino shook his head. "I was too small."

Kino's father laughed. "I remember very well. Oh, how hard you thought it was to be born! You cried and you screamed."

"Didn't I want to be born?" Kino asked. This was very interesting to him.

"You did not," his father told him smiling. "You wanted to stay just where you were in the warm, dark house of the unborn. But the time came to be born, and the gate of life opened."

"Did I know it was the gate of life?" Kino asked.

"You did not know anything about it, and so you were afraid of it," his father replied. "But see how foolish you were! There we were, waiting for you, your parents, already loving you and eager to welcome you. And you have been very happy, haven't you?"

"Until the big wave came," Kino replied. "Now I am afraid again because of the death that the big wave brought."

"You are only afraid because you don't know anything about death," his father replied. "But someday you will wonder why you were afraid, even as today you wonder why you feared to be born."*

We wish to open all possible windows on the subject of death. We do not wish to close our children off from all views except our own. We feel confident that if children build up their own philosophy of what happens at death they will neither go through a period of disillusionment with what we taught them, nor have to outgrow early distorted interpretations of possibly valid adult ideas.

---

*From pages 36-37 of *The Big Wave*, published by the John Day Company (copyright 1947 by the Curtis Publishing Company, 1948 by Pearl S. Buck), reprinted by permission of the author's agent.

14

Sin and Human Nature

"What is a square word, Mummy?"

One way to approach the task of education is to think of it as the process of integrating the new life of the race into the continuing stream of history. Ideally, as children enter into the culture in which they are to live, we would like both to make room for the spontaneity and freshness they bring, and at the same time to enable them to profit by and inherit the best fruits of the experience of past generations.

It is a delicate task to fulfill both of these aims. We do not want the newcomers on the human scene to be overwhelmed by the past. Neither do we want them, through ignorance of the past, to be forced to repeat all of its mistakes and to miss out on its accumulated wisdom.

Children approach life with enormous vitality and with a complete lack of awareness of the patterns of behavior that a culture has evolved in its attempts to enable people to live together harmoniously. As a result, their vitality is often felt as a threat to established ways and hard-won values.

And so, in an attempt to exercise control, most cultures in the past have worked out ways of clamping the lid down on children's energies. They have sought primarily to force children to fit their patterns, and by authoritarian means to compel children to adopt what adults believe to be true, right, and good. Religion and specifically religious education has played an important role in the attempt to make children conform.

A powerful strain in the Judeo-Christian tradition has taught that each new self that comes into the world is essentially sinful. The new self has no awareness of the needs of others and is egocentric. It has no knowledge of the rules of society or the laws of God. The new person is in rebellion against the fathers and most especially against the Supreme Father, God. The sins of the new self must be curbed, and the sinner taught to obey, through a system of rewards and punishments — the final reward being eternal bliss in Heaven, and the final punishment eternal suffering in Hell. The strict religious orthodoxies of today still attempt to control and teach children in this way.

"If you tell a lie, you'll go to Hell," said six-year-old Ruth, with a big question mark in her voice. "Marie said so."

"Oh," said Ruth's mother, "and how does Marie know?"

"Her mother told her so. She told two lies this morning, and her mother said that if she told one more, she would have to stay in Hell an awful long time."

Because this system of controlling human behavior has not worked very well, the theorists have had to say that sin is not only original and universal, but also extremely obstinate. For some reason, even though men are told what is sinful and warned of the dire results of sin, like little Marie they continue to sin.

When an explanation does not explain something, many people feel that a better explanation is called for. At different points down through history, and most spectacularly in the last one hundred years, new theories have been worked out to help account for human conduct. These theories are based on careful observation of human behavior, including the behavior that has been called sinful. These theories, which are still in their infancy, are continually undergoing testing and revision.

An increasing number of social scientists, anthropologists, psychologists, and educators today are convinced that the drive and vitality that children bring onto the scene is neither formless, chaotic, nor essentially self-centered. From birth on, children seem to have very specific needs which vary at different points in their development, and which are not all egocentric. It is the task of the culture to interpret these needs and to try to meet them satisfactorily. What did little Marie need and want that caused her to lie? How could her needs be met so that she would not have to lie? According to our newer theories, children in such situations should have our help, not our condemnation.

For adults not only have misunderstood what motivates children, but also have misunderstood how best to guide them. Authoritatively telling children what they must do, what is right and wrong, or what they must believe, does not seem to be an effective way to help children grow up. Labeling certain actions sinful, having children memorize lists of rules or right actions, threatening them with punishments, does not reach down to the deep roots from which human behavior springs.[1]

One day an eight-year-old boy and a seven-year-old girl were standing by a brook. The boy had a record of long attendance at Sunday school and knew by heart the Ten Commandments.

"Hey, quick, get me a rock," said the boy.

"What for?" asked the little girl.

"There's a frog down on the edge of the water. I want to see if I can hit him."

"Hit him? Why hit him? You'll kill him. Let me go down and see what kind it is," said the little girl.

"Watch out," said the boy as he reached down for a stone and threw it.

This boy had memorized, but not appropriated, the commandment "Thou shalt not kill." The little girl, on the other hand, had never been told, in so many words, that it is wrong to kill. But a long intimacy with nature had made such an action as the little boy's simply unthinkable to her. The beliefs on which children act spring from the heart. These beliefs are based on their own experience, not on rules that are learned "by heart." Beliefs grow from the inside out. If this growth is to take place fruitfully, children need to be allowed to experiment, to test for themselves, to evaluate, in democratically guided groups, various kinds of behavior and various ideas about goodness and truth.

Children need less direction from outside. They need more opportunity to develop self-direction and to gain inner satisfaction — and sometimes dissatisfaction — from the decisions at which they arrive. When human behavior is understood and guided in ways such as suggested here, religion and religious education play a very different role from the role it played when human nature was interpreted differently. Instead of a force to control and hold back vitality, religious education ideally becomes a means of allowing this vitality to flow into the culture without distortion.

Almost without exception, none of us, either as individuals or in families, schools, or social groups, is yet able consistently to provide an ideal learning environment for children. In spite of ourselves, we continue to live in two thought worlds about human behavior. Most of us were raised in the old world of guidance through fear and the use of authoritarian methods. This world is a part of our very personalities and ensnares us, even though we want to inhabit a new world in which an attitude of acceptance prevails, and guidance is through mutual respect and the democratic process.[2]

Many of us hope that, even though *we* are unable to live consistently in this new thought world, our children will come closer to achieving this goal. In order to help bring this about, we are trying, not only to guide our children in these new ways as consistently as we can, but also to en-

courage children to look behind labels, such as "sinful,"
"naughty," and "bad." What are the realities covered up by
these words?

A nine-year-old girl was much annoyed at the cheating
done by one of her classmates. One day she and her mother
were discussing the Roman Catholic practice of confession.

"I think it's a good idea to have confession," said Elizabeth.

"Why?" asked her mother.

"Because it helps to tell people how you feel. *You're* always saying we ought to get out what's bothering us and not
keep it in."

"Yes," agreed her mother, "but confession doesn't always
work that way. It could, I suppose."

"I wonder if Barbara tells the priest when she cheats," said
Elizabeth.

"That's a good example," replied the mother. "If she tells
the priest that she cheats, and if he says that it is bad to do
it and that she mustn't do it any more, I'm not sure that
helps her stop."

"Oh, she knows she's not supposed to. The teacher tells
her that she shouldn't and the priest does too, I guess."

"There must be something Barbara wants so much that
she's willing to cheat to get it," said the mother, thinking.
"If she could talk to one of those doctors I've told you about,
who help people with their mixed-up feelings, maybe she
could find a way to get what she needs without cheating. A
priest could help her do this, but if he says it is bad and
makes her feel ashamed, she probably won't want to tell
what is really bothering her. It will make her want to keep
it inside and cover it up."

Elizabeth laughed and said, "You know what Barbara told
me one day? She said she likes to get into trouble so people
will notice her. She's crazy!"

"Maybe that has something to do with her cheating," suggested the mother. "I know she has a brand-new baby sister and a big sister. Maybe she doesn't get all the attention at home that she would like."

"She always wants to be with smart kids, too," said Elizabeth thoughtfully. "They get to do special things. But she isn't smart."

"Maybe you could try to do things with her when she isn't cheating and showing off," said Mother. "Perhaps she wouldn't feel that she had to do things to get attention so much."

"She isn't going to stop just like that," said Elizabeth doubtfully. "I know her. She wants someone to be noticing her every second."

How right Elizabeth was! This is what the theologians have called the stubbornness of sin. Of course it is stubborn. The child's needs that are being thwarted force her to fly in the face of the standards that the culture has set. The way in which the culture handles these thwarted selves — rewarding the smart, depriving the slow, praising the good, chastizing the bad — simply augments the problems. It is a vicious circle.

Difficult as the task is, we should try to help our children see that even grownups have only begun to understand how human emotions work. Because people have not understood why human beings act as they do, they have not known how to help children or adults to change behavior that bothers other people. They have tried frightening, beating, punishing people who are "bad," "stupid," "different." Now we think other methods are possible.

There is at last a growing body of children's books that seek to help children develop an understanding attitude about human behavior, both their own and that of others. Such stories as "Me Do It" (in *Always Growing*), "Stevie Wasn't Bad" (in *The Family Finds Out*), and "The New Boy at School" (in the third "Martin and Judy" volume) are examples of such stories for five- and six-year-olds. The entire volume *The Tuckers: Growing to Know Themselves* encourages this approach on the five- and six-year-old level. Many of the books for primary age boys and girls written by Jerrold Beim fall in this category too.[3]

The fact that there is an increasing number of such books available stands in marked contrast to the situation in the past, when most children's books written specifically to affect children's behavior were about good children or good animals who were rewarded, and bad children or bad animals who were punished. The young readers were supposed to see what happened to the bad characters and avoid such a fate themselves.

As liberal religious educators, we are still very much in a minority in our attempt not to use moralistic labels either to interpret or to guide children's behavior. Many of our children's friends and teachers, or neighboring adults, still think predominantly in these terms; the adults depend heavily on fear and threat of punishment to guide behavior. These children and adults are able to convey to our children the feeling that certain thoughts or actions are "awful," dreadful, bad, sinful. The air of forbiddenness is related to such things as swearing, going around naked, not believing certain things, not going to church, not belonging to the "right" church, even not being smart. "What would your mother or teacher or God think?" is implied by their shocked expressions.

Many liberal religious parents wonder how they can ground the charge in these remarks, and interpret them to children.

"Mrs. Gleason says it's a sin not to use your brain," reported Tommy, a first-grader. "What's a sin, Ma?"

"Who did she say it to?" asked his mother.

"Oh, Charles Eliot! He's the dumbest kid in the class. He doesn't even know his colors yet!" Tommy's voice was filled with scorn.

"I saw Charles downtown yesterday with his mother. Do you know what?"

"What?" said Tommy.

"His mother is deaf and dumb. That means that she can't hear or talk. They use a special language with their hands to talk to each other. Do you think she's been able to help Charles very much as he was growing up?"

"Gee, I guess not," said Tommy. "Deaf and dumb. Gosh!"

"He's probably way behind most of the first-graders," said Tommy's mother. "He needs extra help in school, and yet Mrs. Gleason has thirty-seven children in the first grade. She just doesn't have time to give him extra help."

"Deaf and dumb. Golly!" And Tommy walked away.

Tommy's mother did not have a chance in this conversation to give the asked-for definition of sin; but she was able to show the little boy that the word was covering up a complex situation. She was able to give him a little sympathetic understanding of that situation.

After a morning spent with three friends, eight-year-old Harvey asked his mother a question.

"Was I baptized when I was a baby?"

"No, you weren't," said his mother.

"Why not?" asked Harvey.

"Well, when you were born I didn't believe in baptizing babies. I felt it was something you could decide for yourself, when you were bigger. I thought it would be like signing you up for Cub Scouts when you were a baby. That would be dumb."

"Why do they baptize babies, anyhow?" asked Harvey. "I'm the only one that isn't." Evidently his friends had given him the feeling that not to have been baptized was pretty serious.

"Different churches teach different things about what baptism means," said his mother, feeling her way uncertainly. "George and John and Ralph all go to the Roman Catholic church. In that church they believe that if a baby isn't baptized right away after it is born, it will go to Hell."

"A little new baby go to Hell? Oh, those guys are always talking about Hell! But they think bad people go to Hell, and what's a baby done that's bad?"

"It's hard to understand how anyone could think that, isn't it," agreed Harvey's mother. "But they believe that everyone who is born has a kind of sickness, which they call sin. And baptism helps to wash it away."

"Does our church think that?" asked Harvey.

"No," replied his mother. "In our church we don't think that. We have a special service, though, at which parents can stand up at the front of the church, with their new babies, and promise to try to do a good job at helping their new child grow up. If I had known about our church when you were born I would have been glad to have you baptized in that way. But I grew up in the church Ralph and George and John go to, and when you were born I knew that I didn't believe all that about sin and Hell."

"Well," said Harvey, still concerned that he was different from his friends, "I wouldn't want to stand up in front of everyone in our church now, especially when the rest of them are babies. But I wish I'd had it done in our church, when I was little."

"You know," said his mother, "in some churches — I think the Quaker church is one — they don't have anything at all like baptism. And in the Baptist church they believe that baptism has to do with things you believe about Jesus, and so they believe that you should be baptized when you're older. So you see, there are lots of different ways to think about baptism."

The mother later commented in her report: "I think Harvey still minded being different from his friends, but at least I think he no longer felt that there was anything bad about him."

In an attempt to interpret the use of the words "sinful" and "bad" to our children, we have also experimented with another approach. We have introduced the idea of the relativity of ethics and social mores at an early age.

A mother was weeding her garden one spring day as her four-year-old son played with two small friends in the sand box. After a little while the four-year-old wandered into the garden.

"What's a square word, Mummy?" he asked.

"A what?" said his mother.

"A square word."

"I'm afraid you'll have to tell me a little more about it. I don't know quite what you're talking about."

"Well, Debbie said that 'phooie' was a square word, and it is very bad to say it."

The mother reports that it finally dawned on her that the children were talking about a "swear word." Then she wondered how one explains to a four-year-old what a swear word is — especially when the example given isn't one. She says that she felt that her child had suddenly come in contact with a totally different approach to life.

If the little boy had been a few years older, his friends would probably have told him that using a swear word is a sin. With children as young as four and five we like to suggest that, just as in our home and our family we have certain ways of doing things, in our part of the world people do some things mostly in one way, but in other places they do them differently. At a little older age we would use the phrase "in our culture." For instance, girls have to wear tops to their dresses in our culture, but they don't in the South Seas. These different ways are thought by some people in each culture to be the only right way. Different peoples have thought that their rules for living together were the best rules, the only rules. Some people still think this way.

To a four- or five-year-old we may suggest that swear

words are words that some people in our part of the world, for a variety of reasons, don't like to hear. In England the word "bloody" is this kind of word, but it isn't in our country. We have other words like "damn" and "Hell." Some children, especially around the ages of six and seven, collect swear words as eagerly as they collect bottle tops and baseball cards. Parents might as well be the ones to introduce the various terms and the degree of shock to grownups that accompanies each one. It is a rather fascinating and difficult job to attempt to give plausible explanations for why each particular word has functioned as a swear word in our culture. If the subject is handled in this calm fashion, most healthy children will conclude that these "treasures" can be stored in a special place with their other treasures and displayed only occasionally.

We might explain, also, that some people use swear words to help get out their mad feelings. Although it may bother other people to hear such words, at least it is better than going around hitting people, or taking one's mad feelings out in more subtle ways.

Now that the world has shrunk so dramatically, and we must have contact with people from all over the world, this broad approach to the patterns of culture is necessary. We are confident that an acquaintance with a variety of culture patterns will not deprive our children of ethical standards, but will contribute to an appreciation of the common human nature that the various cultures have attempted to shape and control. It is this common human nature that all cultures must learn to understand and respect and utilize, rather than suppress and distort.

Only if we are afraid of the dynamic qualities in children's behavior will we feel obliged — like most cultures in the past — to put blinders on children to keep them from discovering that there is more than one way of doing things, and more than one way of believing.

A father and his ten-year-old daughter were discussing the basic difference between an approach to education — and specifically religious education — that encourages personal finding out, testing, questioning, and a dogmatic approach that makes a virtue out of unquestioning acceptance.

"I hope you will never stop wondering and thinking and trying to figure these things out," said the father.

"Well," said the little girl thoughtfully, "nobody can *make* their children stop wondering about things. All the kids can do is not let their parents know they are wondering."

What an adventure those parents are missing!

For it is an adventure to explore religion with children. If we take the time to think through our own ideas and feelings in this important area, we should welcome it as an opportunity rather than a threat when our children come to us with their questions. We will have to draw on all our knowledge of the historic religions, on all our information about child development, and on all our skill in the fine art of communicating with children. Real communication with children is an enterprise that brings its own reward. When we succeed at it, it is for many of us a sacrament.

There will be many times when we miss the mark entirely. One mother found herself using the word "religion" in conversations with her five-year-old son, and realized that the word meant absolutely nothing to the little boy. In an attempt to help him know what she was talking about, she told him one night that religion is about "things that make us wonder." A few days later at supper, the family discussed a neighboring family with three children who never put napkins on the table at meals.

Mother, thinking of her own children's milk-lined lips, said, "I *wonder* how the Browns ever get through a meal without paper napkins!"

A few nights after this, in another bedtime conversation with her five-year-old son, the mother used the word "re-

ligion" again. "Do you remember what I said it meant?"
she asked.

"Oh, yes," replied the little boy, always ready with an answer. "It's about things like how the Browns ever get through
a meal without paper napkins."

The mother chalked up one more failure to communicate.
A tremendous chasm existed between what she knew traditionally belonged in the category of religious "things that
make us wonder," and what her small son, innocent of the
complex phenomenon that is religion, thought might properly belong there. Like this mother, we all tend to be too
eager to hand on to our children the treasures of the race,
and too slow to learn that growth, maturity, and understanding cannot be hurried or coerced.

A young father had a more successful experience with his
eleven-year-old son, Bill. They attended a liberal church.

"Are we Christians?" asked the boy. "Ted says that our
church isn't even Christian because we don't accept Jesus
as our Savior, whatever that means."

"No," said the father, "if that is what makes a church
Christian, we're not Christians."

"Well, are we Jews then?" asked Bill.

"No," said his father, "we're not Jews."

"We surely aren't Buddhists," said the boy, laughing.

"No," said his father, "we aren't Buddhists. But now, ask
me those questions all over again."

A little puzzled, Bill asked, "Are we Christians?"

"Yes," replied his father.

"Are we Jews?"

"Yes."

"Are we Buddhists?"

"Yes."

Bill's eyes twinkled. He understood his father's paradoxi-
cal message: We can learn something from all religious
teachers, adding their best insights to our own.

In the positive religious education of our children, we are seeking to treat religious development as a natural, joyous fulfillment of felt needs and vital interests. This development can be enriched and stimulated by a judicious sharing of the best insights of the entire race, at appropriate points along the way. If we are doing a good job at this, and sharing with children experiences that feed their growing spirits at every level of development, we will not have to be overly worried that our culture seems intent on giving them spiritual indigestion.

With one hand we must seek to minister to the real religious needs of our children, and with the other to interpret traditional religion as it impinges on them. By the time they reach young adulthood we may hope that they will be equipped with a richly nourished religious understanding, firmly based on their own experience and enriched by an appreciative awareness of the religious heritage of men of the past.

Religious education that is an adventure and not an ordeal is still an experiment. But we have high hopes for it.

Notes

Foreword

1. Whitehead, Alfred North, *The Aims of Education* (New York: Mentor Books, 1949), "Freedom and Discipline," p. 50. Quoted by permission of The Macmillan Company.

Chapter 1. *The Culture Will Not Wait*

1. See *The New Beacon Series in Religious Education;* this pamphlet, available from the Division of Education, Council of Liberal Churches (25 Beacon Street, Boston 8, Mass.), describes the books in this series.

Chapter 2. *Our Own Feelings About Traditional Religion*

1. The American Unitarian Association has established both a program of Fellowships (small groups of religious liberals) and the Church of the Larger Fellowship (to which isolated religious liberals may belong by mail). Information may be obtained from 25 Beacon Street, Boston 8, Mass.

Chapter 3. *The Languages of Understanding*

1. Watson, Goodwin, "A Psychologist's View of Religious Symbolism," in *Religious Symbolism,* edited by F. Ernest Johnson (New York: Harper, 1955), p. 123. Quoted by permission of the publisher.
2. Manwell, Elizabeth M., and Fahs, Sophia L., *Consider the Children: How They Grow,* revised edition (Boston: Beacon Press, 1951).
3. Fahs, Sophia L., *Today's Children and Yesterday's Heritage* (Boston: Beacon Press, 1952).
4. Whitman, Walt, *Leaves of Grass and Selected Prose,* Modern Library College Editions, edited by John Kouwenhoven (New York: Modern Library, 1950), page xi. Quoted by permission of Random House, Inc.
5. Whitman, *Leaves of Grass,* p. 217.
6. See Langer, Susanne K., *Philosophy in a New Key* (Cambridge: Harvard University Press, 1942). Many of the ideas in this chapter derive from Mrs. Langer's book. Subsequent quotations are from the Mentor edition (New York, 1948).

7. See Tillich, Paul, "Theology and Symbolism," in *Religious Symbolism*, edited by F. Ernest Johnson (New York: Harper, 1955), p. 116. Dr. Tillich is a theologian who is aware of what has happened to the Christian myth but is reluctant to go beyond it.

8. See Isherwood, Margaret, *The Root of the Matter* (New York: Harper, 1954). This is an interesting and provocative analysis of many of the problems raised in this chapter.

9. Whitman, *Leaves of Grass*, p. 551.

10. Whitman, *Leaves of Grass*, p. 558.

11. Langer, Susanne K., *Feeling and Form* (New York: Scribner's, 1953), pp. 402, 403. Quoted by permission of Charles Scribner's Sons.

12. See, for example, Kenneth Patton's *Hymns of Humanity* (Boston: Meeting House Press, 1951). This hymnbook, which is continually being adapted and developed, demonstrates an imaginative approach to finding new songs. Readings are also available from the Meeting House Press.

Chapter 4. The Younger Child and His Questions

1. Hills, Verna, *Martin and Judy: Playing and Learning*, Vol. III (Boston: Beacon Press, 1943).

2. Storms, Grace, "What Did the Bible Teach?" *Children's Religion*, January 1955.

Chapter 5. The Older Child and His Questions

1. Fitch, Florence M., *One God: The Ways We Worship Him* (New York: Lothrop, Lee and Shepard, 1944).

2. Manwell, Reginald D., and Fahs, Sophia L., *The Church Across the Street* (Boston: Beacon Press, 1947).

3. Dostoevsky, Fyodor, *The Brothers Karamazov* (New York: Random House, Modern Library edition), p. 312. Quoted by permission of the publisher.

4. Wensberg, Katherine S., and Northrop, Mary Myrle, *The Tuckers: Growing to Know Themselves* (Boston: Beacon Press, 1952), p. 107.

5. Evans, Eva Knox, *All About Us* (Irvington-on-Hudson: Capitol, 1952).

6. Edel, May, *The Story of People* (Boston: Little, Brown, 1953).

7. Fahs, Sophia L., *From Long Ago and Many Lands* (Boston: Beacon Press, 1948).

8. Wensberg, *The Tuckers*, p. 123.

Chapter 6. What Kind of Answers?

1. Gesell, Arnold, and Ilg, Frances, *The Child From Five to Ten* (New York: Harper, 1946), p. 433. Quoted by permission of author and publisher.
2. Bradford, Ben, "Rebirth of the Sunday School," *New York Times Magazine*, September 19, 1954. Quoted by permission of the author and the *New York Times*.
3. Langer, *Philosophy in a New Key*, p. 221.
4. Gesell and Ilg, *The Child From Five to Ten*, p. 148.
5. Langer, *Philosophy in a New Key*, p. 237.
6. Whitman, *Leaves of Grass*, p. 25.

Chapter 7. Traditional Teachings About God

1. Tillich, "Theology and Symbolism," pp. 107-108. (Chap. 3, note 7, above.) Quoted by permission of the publisher.
2. One source here was the interesting series on "Christian Teaching and Christian Beliefs," which appeared in *Children's Religion*, from November 1954 through April 1955; *Children's Religion* is published by the Pilgrim Press, Boston. The other sources were confidential reports and miscellaneous reading.

Chapter 8. Interpreting Ideas of God

1. Bradford, "Rebirth of the Sunday School." (Chap. 6, note 2, above.)
2. Hunter, Edith F., *The Family Finds Out* (Boston: Beacon Press, 1951).
3. Hills, *Martin and Judy: Playing and Learning*, Vol. III, p. 44.
4. Hills, Verna, and Fahs, Sophia L., *Martin and Judy: In Sunshine and Rain*, Vol. II (Boston: Beacon Press, 1940), p. 89.
5. Fahs, *From Long Ago and Many Lands*.
6. Gesell and Ilg, *The Child From Five to Ten*, pp. 437-438.
7. Wensberg, *The Tuckers*.
8. Fahs, "The Persevering Ant," in *From Long Ago and Many Lands*, p. 146.
9. Hills and Fahs, "Something New in Judy's Yard," in *Martin and Judy: In Sunshine and Rain*, Vol. II, p. 81.
10. Dodder, G. Clyde, "What Children Think About God," *Children's Religion*, November 1954. Quoted by permission of the author and the Pilgrim Press.
11. Whitman, *Leaves of Grass*, p. 49.
12. Fahs, Sophia L., and Spoerl, Dorothy, *Beginnings of Life and Death* (Boston: Beacon Press, 1938); Fahs, Sophia L., *Beginnings of Earth and Sky* (Boston: Beacon Press, 1937).
13. Gorham, Michael, *The Real Book of American Tall Tales* (New York: Garden City Books, Franklin Watts, 1952).

Chapter 9. New Ways in Prayer

1. Milne, A. A., "Vespers," in *When We Were Very Young* (New York: Dutton, 1924), p. 99. Quoted by permission of the publisher.
2. Gesell and Ilg, *The Child From Five to Ten*.
3. Hollerorth, Hugo J., "What Juniors Think of Prayer," *Children's Religion*, November 1954. Quoted by permission of the author and the Pilgrim Press.
4. Hollerorth, "What Juniors Think of Prayer."
5. Hills, *Martin and Judy: Playing and Learning*, Vol. III.
6. Manwell, Elizabeth, *Always Growing* (Boston: Starr King, 1956). This is a revised edition of Manwell and Fahs, *Growing Bigger*.
7. See Hunter, "A Very First Birthday" and "Mother Learns Not to Be Afraid," in *The Family Finds Out*.
8. Miller, Dessie, "How and What Do Children Pray?" *Children's Religion*, November 1954.
9. See Thomson, Mary M., *Talk It Out With Your Child* (New York: McGraw-Hill, 1953). This is an interesting attempt to bring about "better child guidance through family conversations."
10. See Jenkins, Shacter, and Bauer, *These Are Your Children* (New York: Scott, Foresman, 1949). This book gives a clear, descriptive account of the developmental tasks of growing children.
11. See Bossard, James, *The Sociology of Child Development* (New York: Harper, 1954). This author is keenly aware of the innumerable variables that influence the development of persons. See also Mr. Bossard's *Parent and Child* (University of Pennsylvania Press, 1953).
12. Wensberg, *The Tuckers*.
13. Selections from a book such as Shirley Jackson's *Life Among the Savages* (Permabook edition) can be very relaxing.
14. See Roberts, David, *Psychotherapy and a Christian View of Man* (New York: Scribner, 1950).
15. Jones, Mary Alice, *Tell Me About God* (copyright 1943 by Rand McNally & Company, publishers), p. 52. Reprinted by courtesy of the publishers.
16. Miller, "How and What Do Children Pray?"
17. Aldis, Dorothy, *All Together* (New York: Putnam, 1952). See also McFarland, Wilma, *For a Child* (Philadelphia: Westminster Press, 1947).
18. Thomas, Edith L., *Martin and Judy Songs* (Boston: Beacon Press, 1951). See also Silliman, Vincent, *We Sing of Life* (Boston: Starr King, 1955).

Chapter 10. *Understanding Other Ways of Praying*

1. Baumann, Hans, *The Caves of the Great Hunters* (New York: Pantheon Books, 1954).
2. Armer, Laura A., *Waterless Mountain* (New York: Longmans, Green, 1931).
3. See Ross, Floyd, and Hills, Tynette, *Questions That Matter Most, Asked by the World's Religions* (Boston: Beacon Press, 1954). This book, for older young people and for adults, is useful as an introduction to comparative religious ideas.
4. See Taylor, Florence, *Thine Is the Glory* (Philadelphia: Westminster Press, 1948). This book in the Presbyterian Curriculum series attempts to interpret the Lord's Prayer for primary children. The prayer is also discussed briefly in Chapter 10 of *Jesus the Carpenter's Son* by Sophia L. Fahs (Boston: Beacon Press, 1945), a book for eleven-year-olds and older.
5. Chapter 6, "Life-Symbols: The Roots of Sacrament," in Mrs. Langer's *Philosophy in a New Key*, has an interesting theoretical discussion related to this problem.

Chapter 11. *Interpreting Teachings About Jesus*

1. Hills, Verna, *Martin and Judy: In Their Two Little Houses*, Vol. I (Boston: Beacon Press, 1939), "Baby Sister's Christmas Gift."
2. Manwell, *Always Growing*.
3. Kunhardt, Dorothy, *Once There Was a Little Boy* (New York: Viking, 1946).
4. Fahs, "Stories of Three Great Birthdays," in *From Long Ago and Many Lands*, pp. 176-197.
5. Petersham, Maud and Miska, *The Christ Child* (New York: Doubleday, Doran, 1931).
6. White, Dorothy, *Books Before Five* (New York: Oxford University Press, 1954), p. 184. Quoted by permission of the publisher.
7. Fahs, Sophia L., and Sweet, H. F., *Exploring Religion With Eight-Year-Olds*, revised edition (New York: Harper, 1938), p. 184.
8. Fahs, Sophia L., *Jesus the Carpenter's Son* (Boston: Beacon Press, 1945), Chapter 11.
9. Fahs, Sophia L., *The Old Story of Salvation* (Boston: Starr King, 1955).
10. See Burton and Goodspeed, *A Harmony of the Synoptic Gospels* (New York: Scribner, 1929); Sharman, H. B., *Records of the Life of Jesus* (New York: Association Press, 1917).
11. See *The Abingdon Bible Commentary*, edited by Frederick Carl Eiselen (New York: Abingdon Press, 1929). This is a fairly liberal one-volume commentary.

12. See Sharman, H. B., *Studies in the Records of the Life of Jesus* (New York: Harper, 1938). This is an example of the kind of questioning of the Bible records that might occur in such a study.
13. Smith, Elwyn A., *Men Called Him Master* (Philadelphia: Westminster Press, 1948).
14. Both of these stories appear in Mrs. Fahs's *From Long Ago and Many Lands*.

Chapter 12. Children and the Bible

1. Smart, James D., *The Teaching Ministry of the Church* (Philadelphia: Westminster Press; copyright 1954 by W. L. Jenkins), p. 148. Quoted by permission of the publisher.
2. Smart, *The Teaching Ministry of the Church*, p. 142.
3. For instance, Chapters 6 and 7 of Genesis are an attempt to combine two versions of the Noah legend. Chapters 16-18 of I Samuel are an interesting combination of two stories about David and his relations with Saul.
4. Smart, *The Teaching Ministry of the Church*, pp. 141-142.
5. Klaber, Florence, *Joseph* (Boston: Beacon Press, 1941).
6. Flight, John W., *Moses* (Boston: Beacon Press, 1942).
7. Fahs, *From Long Ago and Many Lands*. "The Jewish Traveler and the Robbers" (the Good Samaritan); "The Very Short Rule" (the Golden Rule); "The Trees Choose a King" (from the book of Judges); "Jesus at a Wedding Party"; "King Saul Finds a Harpist"; "David and Jonathan Become Friends"; "The King's Spear and Water Jug"; "Wise King Solomon"; "The Birth of Jesus."
8. Flight, John, *The Drama of Ancient Israel* (Boston: Beacon Press, 1949).
9. See Miller, Olive B., *A Picturesque Tale of Progress*, Vol. II (Chicago: Bookhouse for Children, 1929), Chapter 1, "Babylonia, The Land of Two Rivers," pp. 11-48.

Chapter 13. The Cycle of Life and Death

1. Hills, "Baby Sister and Sarah the Doll," in *Martin and Judy: In Their Two Little Houses*, Vol. I.
2. Hills and Fahs, *Martin and Judy: In Sunshine and Rain*, Vol. II.
3. Quoted from Leaflet 7, "Trees," in the course *How Miracles Abound* (Boston: Beacon Press).
4. Pratt, Alice D., *Animal Babies* (Boston: Beacon Press, 1941); Hunter, *The Family Finds Out*; Stanger, Margaret, *A Brand New Baby*, revised edition (Boston: Starr King, 1955); Stevens, Bertha, *How Miracles Abound* (Boston: Beacon Press, 1941).
5. Fahs, *From Long Ago and Many Lands*.

6. Fahs and Spoerl, *Beginnings of Life and Death.*
7. *Fireside Book of Folk Songs,* selected and edited by Margaret Bradford Boni (New York: Simon and Schuster, 1947), p. 48.
8. Hills and Fahs, "Judy and Her Father Play a Game," in *Martin and Judy: In Sunshine and Rain,* Vol. II.
9. Wensberg, *The Tuckers.*
10. Fahs, *From Long Ago and Many Lands.*
11. Fitch, Florence M., *Their Search for God: Ways of Worship in the Orient* (New York: Lothrop, Lee and Shepard, 1947).

Chapter 14. Sin and Human Nature

1. See Roberts, *Psychotherapy and a Christian View of Man.* Chapter 4, "The Development of Personal Belief," is an interesting attempt to relate the newer insights to a reinterpreted orthodoxy.
2. See Brogan and Fox, *Helping Children Learn* (Yonkers-on-Hudson: World Book Company, 1955). This book gives many examples of a healthy learning environment.
3. Manwell, *Always Growing;* Hunter, *The Family Finds Out;* Hills, *Martin and Judy: Playing and Learning;* Wensberg, *The Tuckers;* Beim, Jerrold, *The Taming of Toby* (New York: Morrow, 1953). There are many others by Mr. Beim.